DOMAINER'S BIBLE

A Beginner's Guide To Buying and Selling Domain Names

Fifth Edition

Table of Contents

Legal Notices & Disclaimer

The author and publisher have used their best efforts in preparing this book. It is frequently updated, however, due to the constant changes in the domain name industry, readers should keep up with current events and evolutionary changes associated with this business.

The author and publisher do not guarantee the accuracy, effectiveness or applicability of the content found on websites, links, etc., mentioned in this book. This information is provided solely as a service to our readers and they must exercise due diligence and caution regarding anything they read on any website, forum, blog, etc., or in communications with individuals contacted via these sources.

This book is intended to be of an informational nature and is not to be construed as professional business advice that addresses every unique situation associated with each individual reader. Your success in this industry will result entirely from your business skill, financial acumen, domaining related knowledge and sound execution of fundamental tactics and techniques utilized by successful domain name entrepreneurs.

Introduction to Domaining

"Domain names have and will continue to go up in value faster than any other commodity ever known to man."

Bill Gates, CEO – Microsoft

Before we begin I'd like to congratulate you on your decision to purchase the Domainer's Bible. At this moment you are poised to take your first steps into one of the most lucrative investment industries of our time, an industry that has thrived since the early proliferation of the internet and has created no small number of millionaires and even billionaires throughout the course of its existence. The industry I speak of is "Domain Name Speculation", or as it is more commonly known, "Domaining". To put it simply, domaining is the practice of identifying and acquiring valuable domain names, utilizing them to produce recurring revenue streams and ultimately selling them for a sizeable profit.

By delving into the pages of this book you are starting down the exact same path that has taken many people before you into complete financial freedom. You will learn everything from the ground up and glean a crystal clear vision of the most vital aspects of domaining. No matter what your present level of experience is, once you have absorbed the information contained herein you will be equipped with the essential knowledge upon which a successful domaining investment portfolio can be founded.

As a new domainer you should be aware that due to the temperamental nature of Google as a search engine, what works well today might be affected by a Google slap, penalty or a new algorithm change tomorrow and will stop working completely.

While Google updates its search engine algorithms hundreds of times within a year, most of these changes are minor and go on unnoticed. A few updates, however, have the power to impact everyone working online as a domainer, webmaster or SEO specialist regarding site rankings and organic site traffic, rendering many search engine optimization (SEO) techniques useless literally overnight. You will soon learn that the world of SERPS is ever changing and a prominent part of any domaining business.

Here is a list of the most important Google changes that have happened over the years, changes that most seasoned domainers have experienced first-hand.

http://moz.com/google-algorithm-change

What exactly is a domain name?

The most fundamental knowledge that underpins domaining is a clear concept of exactly what a domain name is, beyond the surface level understanding that a typical internet user has. Sure, many people realize that if they type a domain name into an internet browser's address bar they end up at a website, but as a domainer you need to know *how* this process occurs and *why* it offers the investment potential that it does. You don't need to get heavily involved the technical workings of domain names, given that you are an investor and not a technician, but what you do need to learn is everything you possibly can about their *commercial value*. Let's start by drawing an analogy with something I'm sure you are already very familiar with: a real world store in shopping mall. Bear with me while I paint you a picture, the relevance of which will become apparent in just a moment. Harry is a hypothetical businessman that wants to run a shoe store. All his stock is currently sitting in his garage and the first thing he needs is a public location to display it in so that people can come and browse his wares. He rents space from a shopping mall and the physical address of the store he is given is "Shop 3, Level 4, Mega Shopping Mall, Busy St. Burbsville, Somestate 99999". He realizes that no one is ever going to be able to remember that address, and he also wants to build brand awareness, so he registers the business name "Super Shoe Emporium". He moves his stock into the store, hangs his business name over the front door and opens up for business.

Now, if Harry was a webmaster that wanted to run a shoe site the process would be exactly the same. The files of his website are currently sitting on his home PC and the first thing he needs is a public location to display them in so that people can come and browse his site. He rents server space from a web hosting company and the physical address of the space he is given is IP number 118.208.45.214.

He realizes that no-one is ever going to be able to remember that address, and he also wants to build brand awareness, so he registers the domain name "SuperShoeEmporium.com". Then he uploads his website file to his server space, points his domain name to it and opens up for business.

For Harry the shoe store owner his business name becomes a fundamental centerpiece of his success. People can easily look up "Super Shoe Emporium" and find out the physical address they can visit to browse his products. He promotes his business name in all of his marketing and as his branding grows stronger he gets more customers and makes more money. Without his business name precious few people would know about Harry's store, no-one would know how to find it and it would just be a matter of time until his venture failed. But because of the revenue his business name generates, even if Harry shut down his shoe store the name "Super Shoe Emporium" would still have an inherent value all of its own.

For Harry the webmaster the scenario is again exactly the same; his domain name becomes a fundamental centerpiece of his success. People can easily type "SuperShoeEmporium.com" into their web browsers and they will automatically be taken to his website. He promotes his domain name in all of his marketing and as his branding grows stronger he gets more traffic and makes more money. Without his domain name precious few people would know about Harry's website, no-one would know how to find it and it would just be a matter of time until his venture failed. But because of the revenue his domain name generates, even if Harry shut down his website the domain name "SuperShoeEmporium.com" would still have an inherent value all of its own.

When you parallel the value of a domain name to the value of a business name I'm sure the entrepreneurial portion of your brain starts to whir immediately. Just imagine how much money you could make if you could acquire the business name "Coca Cola". You could probably sell neck ties under the name and still enjoy massive revenue. The same principle applies to domain names. Some have an ability to generate revenue that is virtually "plug and play", and trading in these kinds of inherently valuable domain names is what domaining is all about.

What exactly is *domaining?*

Now that you are building a clear concept of exactly what domain names are and why in they can be extremely valuable, your mind is probably already racing around all the possibilities to generate wealth from them. For example, imagine how much money you could make if you could acquire the domain name netbooks.com, or better yet, imagine if you had seen the netbook trend coming and registered the domain before anyone else had thought to do it? Well guess what, a bright spark out there did just that and at present there are approximately 50,000 people per month going through this domain to a site that makes commission every time a netbook sale is referred to Amazon. Commissions from Amazon tend to be around 5% - 8% which is comparable to many retail markup amounts. How much do you think a real world retailer could sell their business name for if they had proof of 50,000 people browsing their products every month? If the owner of this domain decided to sell, you can be sure they would command a very healthy price.

Identifying valuable domain names like this when they are as low in price as possible is the essence of domaining. The actual creation of domain names costs only a few dollars so the highest profits come from being the very first person to own a domain that goes on to become highly commercially relevant. For example, the highest purchase price for a domain in recorded history was almost $10,000,000 for fund.com in March 2008. Compare this sale amount to a typical domain registration fee of around $10. Despite the fact that this transaction holds the record for the highest domain sale amount of all time, in what other investment industry could you find even one example of an asset increasing in value by a factor of *one million*? You might need to read that one more time. Yes, I said that this domain became *one million* times more valuable since its creation, and the chances are its value will only continue to escalate.

One of the most incredible aspects of domaining is that is accessible to people from all walks of life. Unlike the stock market or real estate, you can start building your domain portfolio even with just a modest initial investment budget, and yet astute investors have still reported profits comparable or even greater than typical stock market and real estate investment returns. Domaining does have one key thing in common with other investment industries however, and that is the fact that sound decisions lead to profits while poor decisions lead to losses. This means that as a domainer you are in the business of *making sound decisions*. To make sound decisions what you need is a clear picture of what makes a domain name valuable so you can identify the opportunities that are likely to make you money and avoid those that are likely to cause losses. Through this book you are going to discover the essential information that all successful domainers understand, so you can start building a profitable domain portfolio and create financial freedom for you and your loved ones.

Domain Name Basics

As I mentioned earlier you don't need to dig too deeply into the technical side of domain names for the purpose of becoming an educated investor, however there are a few basic elements of their operation that you will need to be aware of. A car salesman doesn't need the technical knowledge that a mechanic has, but still needs to understand certain aspects of what makes a vehicle work. The same principle applies to trading in domain names. You don't need to know the ins and outs of absolutely everything going on under the hood of a domain, but there are a few key areas you should have a basic understanding of.

The Domain Name System

As you are probably aware the internet is comprised of an enormous number of computers connected together to form a vast network that spans the globe. This immense network and the resources it contains are structured into a well-organized hierarchy of levels called the Domain Name System (DNS). It is this tree like system that allows for the lightning quick communication we have come to know in today's internet. Every single website occupies a unique position in this hierarchy and a domain name describes its exact location.

Each level of the Domain Name System is divided into parts and labeled. The highest level of the system is divided into parts called Top-level Domains (TLDs). The most well-known of these Top-level Domains bears the label "com", a name that was originally given to this section of the internet intended to host websites of a *commercial* nature. Two more prominent Top-level Domains are labeled "net" and "org". TLD labels are commonly known as "domain name extensions" and at present there are approximately 280 of these extensions in existence.

Creation and labeling of Top-level Domains is controlled by the Internet Corporation for Assigned Names and Numbers (ICANN), a non-profit corporation that was established in 1998 to oversee the Domain Name System. Whilst ICANN delegates responsibility for actually managing TLDs to other organizations, they have the sole power to decide if new TLDs will be created and what they will be labeled. If an interest group wishes to have a new TLD created they must submit their proposal to ICANN and lobby for their cause.

Each Top-level Domain is again divided into smaller parts and labeled. Given that these divisions occur at the second level of the "tree" that makes up the Domain Name System they are called Second-level Domains (SLDs). Unlike TLDs the creation and labeling of SLDs is largely open to members of the public. You will know the process of creating and labeling SLDs by a more simple expression: registering a domain name.

A full domain name is actually comprised of the labels that signify where it sits in the Domain Name System, and those labels are connected together by dots. The right-most label is always the Top-level Domain, which is why every website address ends in "com", "net" or whichever label it falls under. To the left of that is the Second-level Domain, for example google.com. An additional label to the left would signify a third level in the domain hierarchy, for example mail.google.com. Third-level domains like this are commonly referred to as "subdomains". Even the familiar "www" prefix is actually just a subdomain. In fact, you don't even have to use "www" in your domain name and it is the standard only because we have grown accustomed to using it. In reality you can use any subdomain you choose which is why you see some websites with prefixes like "www2" or "secure". You can actually keep adding labels to the left and descend up to 127 levels into the Domain Name System however there is rarely if ever any reason to do so.

As a domainer, you will be primarily concerned with two of the levels in the Domain Name System; the top-level and the second-level. You can't create your own Top-level Domains but you can create your own Second-level Domains and choose which TLD to create them within. Again, this is more commonly referred to as registering a domain name. Becoming the registered owner of a second level domain effectively means you control a specific segment of the Top-level Domain it is a part of. Territory within certain Top-level Domains is in higher demand than others. For example, "com" domain names are almost always more coveted than "info" domain names. Additionally, certain TLDs are accessible only to residents of particular countries or to certain kinds of organizations. The following section describes the different kinds of TLDs and the restrictions that surround them.

Generic Top-level Domains (gTLDs)

Generic Top-level Domains always have labels with three or more characters. The first of these gTLDs, created in 1984, were "com", "edu", "gov", "mil", "org" and "net". Since then additional gTLDs have been created to accommodate the growth and changing nature of the internet.

Unrestricted gTLDs

Unrestricted gTLDs are available for registration by any person for any purpose. The policies that govern these domains come directly from ICANN rather than having been delegated to another organization. The most prominent gTLDs are "com", "net", "org", "info" and "co". The fact that these domains have unrestricted access makes them the gTLD of greatest interest to domainers. Registration and trade of these domains goes on under the most freedom of any kind of domain and traditionally the majority of domaining has been within the area of unrestricted gTLDs.

The ".co" domain extension is a relatively new addition to the domain names family and it was quite successfully launched for general registration in 2010. It is overall well liked because it is short, memorable and easily recognizable, however at this time the extension ".com" is still the first one with over 80 million registered domains to date.

See Appendix A for a full list of unrestricted gTLDs

Sponsored Top-level Domains (sTLDs)

Sponsored Top-level Domains (sTLDs) are domains have rules established by private organizations that restrict their registration. These private organizations are referred to as the "sponsors" of the domain in question hence the term *Sponsored* Top-level Domains. sTLDs tend to represent particular industry groups or sectors of government. For example, the "museum" gTLD is sponsored by the Museum Domain Management Association on behalf of the International Council of Museums. As I'm sure you can guess, access to this gTLD is restricted to museums and museum professionals.

For the most part, sTLDs are of little consequence to domainers given the heavily controlled restrictions in accessing them.

See Appendix B for a full list of sTLDs

Country Code TLDs (ccTLDs)

Where a gTLD has three characters or more a Country Code TLD (ccTLD) always has exactly two characters and represents a specific country or territory. For example, the ccTLD for the United States is "us". There are over 240 ccTLDs currently in existence. The management and allocation of a ccTLD is typically handled by the host nation. In some countries instead of allowing the more typical second level domain registration only third level domain registration is permitted. For example, in the United Kingdom members of the public cannot register a domain under "uk", only under "co.uk" or "org.uk".

Some nations prohibit the use of their particular ccTLD by foreign entities, while others require that registrants be citizens. Those ccTLDs with less rigorous access requirements can make excellent investment opportunities for domainers, as can a ccTLD in one's own country of residence. In fact, with the ever increasing levels of competition in the gTLD space, many investors are turning their focus to ccTLDs with talk of them having a prominent role to play in the future of domaining.

There are a number of attractive advantages that ccTLDs have over gTLDs:

Geographical focus

A geographically-focused domain name can help to specifically target the marketplace of a certain region. Some search engines will give preference to ccTLD domains in geo-targeted web searches, and this can help to attract more traffic from a particular location. Using a ccTLD can also appeal to national sentiment by making a website appear as though it is locally owned and managed.

Availability of domain names

Within the highest demand gTLDs many of the most potentially lucrative domains have already been registered and are only available for acquisition by those with extremely deep pockets. However within certain ccTLDs a great many valuable domain names are still available for registration. Additionally, certain existing ccTLDs may be far less costly to acquire than their gTLD counterparts. You may be able to buy five ccTLDs for the same amount as one gTLD of the same name, and yet be able to grow those five domains into assets that generate a high amount of revenue overall due to their geotargeted nature.

Language

Obviously there are billions of people in the world for whom English is not their first language, however gTLD based websites tend to be dominated by the English language. Using specific ccTLDs can help to flag a website as offering content in the first language of a certain target market. Again, this ability to laser target a specific group of people offers great potential for those who wish to market to such groups instead of to the entire world at once.

Commercial and vanity ccTLDs

Certain ccTLDs have become as open to registration as unrestricted gTLDs are. Such ccTLDs have become known as commercial or vanity domains in reference to the most common reasons for their use outside of the related country. A number of the world's smallest countries have licensed access to their ccTLDs and use the royalty payment to supplement their economies. A well-known example is that of the island of Tuvalu, who in 2000 established an agreement with VeriSign to be paid $50 million in royalties across a twelve year period for commercial access to their "tv" domain extension.

See Appendix C for full list of ccTLDs and Appendix D for a list of commercial and vanity ccTLDs.

Restrictions on valid SLDs

While certain TLDs allow registrations from any person, there are still only certain formats of second-level domain that will be accepted. The elements of a valid domain name are:

- May contain numbers ranging from 0-9
- May contain letters from A-Z
- May contain hyphens (-) but may not start or end with a hyphen
- May contain a total of 67 characters (any combination of the above)

Domain names are typically registered in lower case letters. Doing otherwise has been known to produce technical and legal problems in the past and you would be wise to avoid the use of upper case letters when registering a domain name.

Domain Name Registrars

While members of the public do have access to register domains under specific TLDs there is one restriction that applies in all circumstances: all domain registrations must be processed by accredited companies known as Domain Name Registrars. gTLD registrars can only be accredited directly by ICANN and ccTLD registrars must be accredited by the relevant authority for each country or territory. For each TLD the entire list of its registered domains is stored in a database called a Domain Name Registry. Each of these databases is controlled by a specific Registry Operator. For example, the "com" registry is operated by VeriSign. Only accredited Domain Name Registrars have access to interact with Registry Operators and ICANN, and to change and update the records in the Domain Name Registries.

For example, when an end user registers a "com" domain through the accredited registrar GoDaddy, the company then pays a maximum of US$6.86 to VeriSign annually and an admin fee of US$0.20 to ICANN. They then have the right to update the Domain Name Registry records for that domain. It is only the strict control over changes to the Domain Name Registries that ensures domains have only one owner at any given time, and that information on where each domain points to (IP address mapping) is consistent across the entire internet.

A number of registrars also provide access to registration through resellers. Domain name resellers are provided with access to the registrar's infrastructure and given lower registration fees than the general public. They then have the option of generating sales of domain registrations and putting their own markup onto the fees. The reseller keeps the markup amount and the domain registration is then actually processed through the registrar they act as a "front end" for.

At the time a domain name registration is purchased through a registrar, the following transaction details are recorded in the Domain Name Registry:

- Domain name
- Registrant name (or company name)
- Registrant address and other contact information
- Date of purchase
- Duration of registration (1-10 years)

One important factor to remember is that although we speak of owning a domain name, the reality is that when you register a name you are entering into an agreement that is more akin to a lease than an outright purchase. The registrar you go through pays annual fees for your domain to ICANN and the appropriate Registry Operator, so you can be sure those fees will be passed on to you every year. The exact amount you will be charged depends on the markup your registrar loads onto their registration fees. You have the right to control a domain name for only as long as you pay its annual "lease" fees, with a maximum registration period of ten years. Eventually, you must renew the registration or decide to let it lapse.

Another important detail to remember is that because you do not own a domain name outright, under certain conditions a registrar or a court of law may terminate your right to its usage. An example of where this might occur is if you use a company's trademark in your domain without the legal right to do so. In the early days of domaining a popular strategy was to register the domain of a trademark before anyone else could get to it, and then to sell that domain to the trademark owner. Another similar tactic was to register a slightly misspelled version of the trademark, known as a "trademark typo domain". Rules and regulations have evolved since then however and an individual organization can file a complaint with ICANN if they believe a registrant is infringing their intellectual property rights. There is also the possibility that lawsuits may be made against domain registrants seen to be infringing rights to a trademark. For these reasons the practice of domainers registering trademark domains has all but died out.

See the Appendix section for a full list of gTLD Registry Operators and ICANN Accredited gTLD Registrars.

How to Make Money Domaining

Now that you have a foundation in the essential mechanics behind domain names we can move on to what is of course the most important part of domaining: the method by which you make money. Profits from domaining don't come from a single step; rather they come from a complete investment process. There are four basic components to the overall process of domaining.

- Domain valuation and acquisition
- Generating revenue from domains while you own them
- Domain development
- Selling domains for a profit, also called domain flipping

The second and fourth components in this list are the ones through which your domains pay dividends; generating revenue from domains you own and selling domains to investors. If you know the market well enough you can skip the second and third components all together with suitable domains and simply sell them immediately after purchase. These kinds of fast turnaround sales are referred to as flipping and can be an excellent source of revenue but require an understanding of which domains are appropriate for this process and which marketplaces to buy and sell in. The following sections will take a closer look at what is involved in each one of the four key components of domaining.

COMPONENT 1: Domain valuation and acquisition

Whether you intend to flip domains, earn revenue while you own them or to develop them in any way, you can't progress until you actually add some domains to your portfolio. There are two ways for you to do this:

- Creating new domains
- Purchasing existing domains

Typically creating a new domain is quite inexpensive with ".com", ".net" and ".org" domains averaging around $10 to register and ".info" domains at around $3. Commercialized ccTLDs such as ".tv", ".ws" and ".bz" are usually around $30. Existing domains will typically be more expensive than new ones as there may already be value attached to them, or simply because a current owner may only be willing to sell for a certain amount.

Whether you are creating new domains or purchasing existing ones you will need to keep in mind that your goal is to make money from them. In either case you will need to understand what does and does not constitute existing or potential value in a domain name so you can make wise investments. We will cover this subject at length further on.

COMPONENT 2: Revenue while you own a domain

The primary method of generating revenue from a domain while you own it is via advertising. There are a number of different forms of advertising revenue you can tap into but the two most common for domainers are as follows.

Pay per click parking

Pay per click (PPC) is a form of advertising, usually in a text based format, whereby the advertiser is charged only when a person clicks on their ad, effectively generating a lead for their business. These kinds of ads are almost all carried by individual website owners who are paid every time a visitor to their site clicks on one of the PPC ads they are hosting. A common practice for domainers is to place a landing page with an arrangement of PPC ads on the domains they own. It is typical for a certain percentage of people that arrive on the landing page to click on the ads and generate revenue for the domain owner.

Affiliate programs

Affiliate programs are still a form of advertising, however instead of being paid when a person clicks on an ad you are paid when you refer an actual sale to an advertiser. Advertisers usually pay a percentage based commission and the amounts tend to be higher than individual PPC payments but lower in frequency. An alternative to PPC landing pages is to instead present a selection of offers or advertising for relevant affiliate programs.

COMPONENT 3: Developing domains

If a domain shows significant potential and you feel you can add a sizeable amount to your earnings, you may elect to develop a domain by having a custom revenue generating website created for it. The downside to relying solely on PPC or affiliate programs is that quite often a large portion of the actual revenue goes to the advertiser and the network they purchased their ads through.

For this reason many domains choose to develop their most promising domains into something more in depth than a simple landing page. Adding a website or forum to a domain can be time consuming and expensive so it is important that the prospects selected for such a process have a high probability of generating increased returns.

COMPONENT 4: Selling – the end goal

As with any endeavor you need to understand what your ultimate goal is before you can work towards it. In the case of domaining the goal you should keep in mind is to eventually sell every domain you acquire for maximum profit. You may earn excellent revenue from domains while you own them but you should always work to ensure you can sell any domain in your portfolio at the moment you want or need to. A key factor in any business should be a path to liquidity, so for every domain you purchase you should consider right from the outset how you will go about selling it. The only way you can ensure all of your domains have solid potential for eventual resale is to understand what it is that makes them valuable.

When it comes to selling your domain (if this business model appeals to you), there are a few marketplaces worth checking out, along with a few domainer forums including established marketplace sections:

- www.NamePros.com
- www.Sedo.com
- www.Godaddy.com
- www.Ebay.com
- www.Flippa.com
- www.Dnforum.com

See the Appendix section for a full list of domain marketplaces.

One of the newcomer marketplaces for selling and buying virtual properties is Flippa.com. While new and established websites constitute the site's main business, there are more and more domains that show up in daily listings, which makes it worthwhile considering it as a viable source of domain flipping income.

Domain Flipping

Domain flipping is a niche within the domaining business, which consists of buying domains at a low price and selling them at a profit within a short time. With domain flipping you only keep the domains in your possession for a little while. There is a quick turnaround between buying the domain and reselling it on the market. The whole intent of buying a domain is for flipping it as fast as possible at the highest price, even if the profit is less than when engaging in long term domain investing.

Understanding the value of a domain

In order to sell domains for the highest possible amount you need to understand what characteristics make them valuable in the eyes of potential buyers. When you understand these characteristics the pre-sale components of domaining become clearer:

Identify and acquire domains with the highest level of potential and existing resale value characteristics.

During ownership, realize potential resale value characteristics through developing and generating revenue from the domain.

As mentioned earlier you can't be a domainer until you add some domains to your portfolio. However, you can't make good acquisition decisions until you know how to identify potential and existing resale value characteristics. The following section will teach you what these characteristics are and show you exactly how to find them.

Domain Value Characteristics

The key that underpins the assessment of any domain's value is one simple question:

- How much revenue can the domain generate?

As with any investment opportunity the number one focus is the bottom line. This may seem obvious now but when you start to immerse yourself in the finer points of domaining it can become only too easy to lose sight of the forest for the trees. Avoid getting distracted by complexities and remind yourself to keeping coming back to this one vital question. Unless you know how much revenue a domain can generate, it is essentially worth nothing to you.

Revenue x Traffic

Prior to selling a domain name, revenue comes in one way only: through traffic and the revenue that traffic generates. To put it simply the revenue generated by a domain is largely determined by:

- The average revenue per visitor multiplied by the number of visitors.
- Therefore to evaluate the revenue generation potential of any domain you need only answered the following two queries:
- What average revenue can be generated per visitor?
- How many visitors can the domain draw?

It is crucial to realize that the highest value domains have a strong answer to both of those questions. Additionally you must always speculate on the average revenue a domain can generate per visitor before you consider the amount of traffic it can draw. Often people get the false idea that any domain that can draw a large amount of traffic is highly valuable by default. This is not the case, as all the traffic in the world is worthless if it does not generate any revenue. In fact, a high traffic domain that generates little to no revenue can even end up with negative worth if its maintenance costs are not covered.

For example, you might get what seems like a fantastic domain name that puts you at the top of the traffic heap for "free stuff for broke people". You might get a phenomenal number of visitors to this hypothetical domain, but then face unexpected costs to support the high amount of traffic. You might then also find that you are generating no revenue because the people the domain attracts don't want to spend any money. Bear in mind that it is people who are in the process of shopping online who are most likely to pay attention to advertising. People who have no money to spend will typically ignore advertising all together. In this scenario the low average revenue per visitor translates to a low value domain despite the high levels of traffic. Remember, zero dollars multiplied by one million is still zero dollars.

This is why the very first question you should ask of any domain is "What average revenue can be generated per visitor?" What you should be looking for is domains that have the highest amount of commercial relevance. The more directly relevant a domain is to a specific area of commerce the more likely it is to be lucrative. For example, an outstanding domain to own would be creditcards.com because it relates directly to the credit card industry and will attract traffic that is highly likely to generate revenue. Credit card companies pay very well for quality leads and there would be few reasons for a person to visit a credit card site if they weren't in the process of choosing one to apply for. These factors combine to suggest this domain is likely to generate excellent average revenue per visitor.

Once you have established that a domain has good revenue potential then the question of traffic potential becomes relevant. If you know a domain can generate a certain amount per person, then every extra visitor translates to extra revenue. With the example of creditcards.com there are a number of factors, which will be explained in depth further on, that make this domain a virtual traffic magnet. At the time this book was written, this domain ranked second in a US focused Google search for "credit card" coming second only to Google's own related news results. It even outranks all of the actual credit card company websites. According to compete.com it receives approximately one million visitors a month. The high average revenue per visitor multiplied by the high number of visitors makes it an excellent example of a highly valuable domain.

Bear in mind when considering this example that this domain is in the top echelon of highly valuable domains. As a beginner in domaining you will most likely need to set your sites a little lower so you can get the ball rolling. It is easier to make $10 each from 100 domains than $1000 from a single domain. The thing to remember is that commercial relevance is on a sliding scale. Every domain you invest in does not have to be 100% commercially relevant. As long as a domain is commercially relevant in some way you have the opportunity to turn a profit. Your goal is to identify the most commercially relevant domains available to you at any given time. As you build up your portfolio and the amount of capital you have to invest, options will open up to you to break into those upper echelons of highly valuable domains.

While the questions of revenue and traffic potential are of fundamental importance, you still will not need to labor too intensively over them when you make your initial assessment of a domain. The reason for this is that it's only if you are going to actually develop a domain that you need to get into low level specifics and very precise numbers. As a domainer you simply won't have the time to do an extremely thorough analysis of every single domain you buy. A high level forecast will suffice and once you become familiar with the value characteristics of domains you will be able to assess their potential quite quickly.

Remember that valuation should always come before acquisition of a domain name unless you want to learn the hard way by losing money on poor investment choices. Before you even thinking about spending a cent on any domain name you need to understand the valuation process. The following sections, each title prefixed with "Domain Valuation", will teach you this process so that when you come to actually making purchases you will know what you need to consider. You can apply this process either to ideas you have for new domains or to existing domains you are considering acquiring.

Domain Valuation: Assessing Revenue Potential

Remember that the key to evaluating the potential for revenue generation is to ask what level of commercial relevance any given domain has. This can be determined by running through the following four questions. Again, you don't need to labor intensively over these questions but you should at least have a high level answer to each one. I'm going to use an obscure and somewhat random domain as an example to show you how adaptable this process is: "raisebabychickens.com". The process assumes you have no information about any existing revenue patterns for the domain. If you are buying an existing domain, check out whether the current owner can provide records of revenue history and if so, simply perform the following process to help verify the information given to you.

1. What industries does the domain's traffic relate to?

If a domain is going to generate revenue that money has to come from somewhere. As much as we'd like people to, they don't tend to give us money for no reason. A domain has the ability to generate revenue when person or organization in a certain industry is willing to pay for advertising exposure or referred sales. Therefore the first step to evaluating revenue potential is to ask what industries the domain relates to in which people are willing to buy advertising or offer commission.

In some cases you may think a domain relates to no particular industries at all but be careful not to jump to that conclusion too quickly. For example, consider what you would think if offered an opportunity to purchase a domain related to donating cars to charity? At first you would probably think that there is no industry related to this topic as it focuses on charity rather than profit. You would probably also think that few people would be willing to spend money on advertising related to this topic.

What would you then think if you were told that customers of Google Adwords pay up to $44 per click for traffic related to the keywords "donating a used car"? Yes, you read that correctly – at present people are paying $44 for every single click through they get on this subject. This example demonstrates that you should never assume anything about the value of a domain name or the topic it relates to until you have the chance to do a little research.

One of the easiest and most reliable ways you can see what industries might relate to a given domain is to use the Google Adwords Keyword Planner Tool. You can access this tool free of charge via the following link:

https://adwords.google.com/ko/KeywordPlanner/Home

Up until recently the main free keyword tool was Google Adwords Keyword Tool, however Google has recently phased it out and replaced it with the Keyword Planner. This tool is a combination of the Keyword Tool and Traffic Estimator.

In order to use the Keyword Planner, you need to be logged on to your Adwords account, which makes it one of the visible differences between the two tools: previously you could use the Keyword Tool without being logged on to your account, however you would only get 100 results. Being logged on to Adwords allows you get as many as 800 keywords with one single keyword search.

If you don't have an Adwords account, it is easy and free to sign up. You will need an email address (it doesn't have to be Gmail). You can follow the steps to create your account at:

https://accounts.google.com/ServiceLogin?service=adwords

Once you are logged in to your Adwords account, you can access the Keyword Planner tool at:

https://adwords.google.com/ko/KeywordPlanner/Home

To start searching for relevant keywords, click on Search for keywords and group ideas.

This will give you the option to add an initial seed phrase made of single word keywords, such as: home, car, wedding, holiday, etc, or two word keywords such as: wedding favors, car mortgage, home improvement, etc.

The result will be a list called Keywords (by relevant) of 800 keywords. Click on the column Avg. monthly searches to filter the data from the highest searched to the lowest searched keywords, and then click on the Download button at the top to download the data to your computer for further filtering in order to find those gem keywords that will become your winning domains or will help you choose the industry that you want your domain to be part of.

2. Are monetization options are available?

We discussed earlier that the two primary means of generating revenue from a domain you own are PPC advertising and affiliate programs. Once you know what industries relate to a domain name you then need to discover if there are active PPC advertisers and affiliate programs within those industries.

Research Method: Active PPC advertisers

The first step to establishing if there are active PPC advertisers has already been taken when you used the keyword suggestion tool to check the industries related to your domain. You will see there is a column in the results headed "Advertiser competition" under which there are small bars filled with green to differing degrees. The more full these bars are the more people are advertising under the respective keyphrases. In the top results for this search the advertising competition is rated between "average" to "very high" which is an indication there are active advertisers at present. You may not actually use Adsense on your domains but nonetheless the Adwords research tool can be used to gauge the approximate level of PPC advertiser activity in a particular area.

Research Method: Active affiliate programs

Assessing the presence of affiliate programs within the industry is a fairly simple affair. The easiest method is to simply perform a Google search for the keyphrases you identified as relating to industries along with the word "affiliate". For example, "chicken pens affiliate", or "chicken supplies affiliate". In the results of the search for "chicken pens affiliate" three of the first four listings were for programs paying commission on sales of ebook guides to chick pen building. For "chicken supplies affiliate" the first listing was for a program paying commission on various kinds of poultry supplies.

Another method you can use is a search of Clickbank, a large affiliate network for the sale of non-physical items such as ebooks. You can access the marketplace here:

https://accounts.clickbank.com/account/marketplace.htm

Note: You do need to be logged on to your Clickbank account to use the marketplace feature.

Once logged on, go to the Marketplace and use the "Find products" search bar to see if there are any related items you can earn commission on. Start by searching for the words that make up your domain name, in this case "raising baby chickens". This search returns three ebooks on raising chickens with each one paying commission on referred sales. Then search for the keywords related to the industries you identified earlier. A search for "chicken pens" returns five guides to chicken coops on the first page of results.

These three tests have shown us that there are active monetization options available for this particular domain. You can perform these tests on any domain you are evaluating.

3. What payouts do the available monetization methods offer?

Our Adwords suggestion tool results earlier indicated that PPC advertisers are currently spending up to $1.60 per click within the related industries. Bear in mind that as the host for PPC ads you only get a certain percentage of the overall revenue your domain generates. Most of the advertising revenue goes to the company that manages the ad network, such as Google or Yahoo, and if you are using a domain parking service they will keep some of the remaining revenue as well. As a very approximate rule of thumb, the ad network keeps around 90% of PPC revenue and the remaining 10% goes to you if you create your own PPC landing pages. If you use a domain parking service this left over amount will be split between you and them, with you typically keeping 60%.

Research Method: PPC payout

- To figure out what the approximate click revenue is for a keyphrase divide the CPC by 10

Example: "chicken pens" CPC = $1.60

$1.60 / 10 = 16c

- If you will be using a parking service, figure out roughly what portion of the revenue you will keep by multiplying it by 0.6

Example: "chicken pens" revenue = 16c

16c x 0.6 = 9.6c

To give you a frame of reference, the very top of the PPC scale has advertisers paying $60 to $100 per click. These high end ads would generate between $4 and $10 per click in revenue for you but exist only within extremely high competition areas such as debt consolidation, insurance and credit cards. A more typical payout range is 6c to 55c. This tells us that at 9c – 16c the PPC ads related to our example domain would fall into the lower end of the typical payout spectrum but still be within the expected average.

Research Method: Affiliate program payout

In the previous step we discovered there are affiliate programs relevant to raising chickens, chicken pens and chicken supplies. Now we want to find out how much these programs are paying. For the programs found via Google, simply click through to the page listed in the search results and read about the affiliate program. The first affiliate program that appeared in our results stated it pays $12.34 per sale. The second offered up to $35. For the programs found through Clickbank the payouts will be listed right there in the search results. The commissionable products returned in the search we performed earlier were paying between $8 and $27 per sale.

The important thing to remember with affiliate programs is that unlike PPC you don't get paid unless a person clicks on the ad you are hosting and goes on to buy the product. A good rule of thumb is to estimate that for every 100 people that click on an affiliate ad 1 person will buy a product, i.e. a 1% conversion rate. If you have information on what the conversion rate actually is you can use it for your estimates, otherwise 1% is a good approximate amount to default to. This conversion rate translates to effectively mean that every click you get generates an average of 1% of whatever commission rate you are being paid.

• To figure out the approximate click revenue for an affiliate program divide the commission amount by 100

Example: Clickbank ebook commission = $35

$35 / 100 = 35c

In summary, for our example domain we have estimated PPC and affiliate programs can generate earnings per click (EPC) of approximately 8c – 35c.

4. What click through rate can be expected?

Once you have approximated the amount of revenue each click will generate, you want to know roughly what percentage of your traffic is likely to click on your ads. This percentage is known as the Click Through Rate (CTR). CTR can depend on many different factors such as page layout, the type of industry and the type of offer, however the average CTR for a PPC landing page tends to be around 15% - 35%. For the purpose of your estimations, assume the CTR will be on the lower end of the spectrum. This way if your CTR is low you are prepared.

In practical terms, a 15% CTR means that 15 in every 100 people will click on your advertisements. In the case of our "raising baby chickens" domain this means that for every 100 visitors, 15 people will generate 8c – 35c each. In other words, for every 100 visitors the domain attracts it should earn approximately $1.20 to $5.25.

Overall revenue potential

As a result of the research conducted, our final assessment of approximate revenue potential for this example domain is:

$1.20 - $5.25 per 100 visitors

Remember when you perform your own assessments of potential revenue that this is a very approximate process. There will always be factors that are very difficult to include in such an evaluation so treat this as a "ball park" figure of the possible earnings. Once you run through this process a few times you will be able to perform it very quickly so that you don't get bogged down in the details. Also, remember that it only takes revenue of 2c per day for you at least cover costs on a $10 domain registration. In the case of our example domain this would mean only two visitors a day would be required. Even low revenue generating domains can lead to profit.

Domain Valuation: Assessing Traffic Potential

Once you know the approximate revenue that can be generated by visitors to a domain, the next question is how many visitors can it draw? For example, we estimated "raisebabychickens.com" could generate between $1.20 and $5.25 per 100 visitors. Therefore if this domain could draw just 25 visitors per day it would generate $109 to $479 per year. At first this may not seem like much, but if you had 250 equivalent domains you would be earning $27,375 to $119,765 per year even from relatively low traffic and earnings per click. Just an extra 5 visitors per day to each of your domains would add another $5475 to $23,953 to your annual income. It is clear from this example why it is once you have estimated revenue potential that traffic potential becomes truly important.

Understanding Traffic Flow

There are essentially two ways a person can arrive at a domain. They can either type the address directly into their browser address bar or they can click on a referring link.

Type in traffic can come either by a person deliberately typing or accidentally mistyping a domain name. Domains designed to capture deliberate type in traffic are referred to as "Type-in" domains whereas those designed to capture common mistypings' are known as "Typo" domains.

Referring links can come either from websites or from search engines. Links to a domain from another website are called "backlinks" and "link popularity" is a measurement of the overall weight of those backlinks. Links in a search engine's results are known as "indexed pages."

The following outline provides some of the pros and cons of each different type of traffic:

Type-In Domains

Description
- Users navigate to a Web site by typing the site address directly in the browser

- The site address usually consists of common words that represent the services or products the site provides, such as, *cars.com*

Pros

- Provides direct navigation to the site
- Search engine is not needed to locate the site
- Generates high traffic flow
- Some studies show that sales from visits are generally higher from type-in traffic or bookmarks than those that come from search engines

Cons

- Most type-in domains are taken
- Those that are available for purchase are quite expensive
- Typo Domains

Description

- Visitors arrive on a landing page on a typo domain, for example, *carrs.com* because they mistype the site address
- The typo landing site may contain links to the sought after site, such as *cars.com*

Pros

- Usually more affordable than type-in domains

- Can leverage the popularity of other domains

Cons

- Care must be taken not to breach trademarks or other intellectual property so as to avoid lawsuits

Link Popularity

Description

- Total number of Web sites that link to your site.
- Determines how popular a site is based on the number of incoming links from other sites

Pros

- Plays an important role in the visibility of the site and where it ranks in search engine results

Cons

- Backlinks may not be permanent. The traffic that flows from them can recede over time
- Visitors following old links may leave quickly of site content has changed, eg. to a PPC landing page

Search Engine Indexing

Description

• Pages of your site that have been indexed by a search engine and may be delivered in search results

• Coming up in search engines often depends on keywords, both in the domain and on the site itself

Pros

• Can bring traffic to domains unlikely to get type-in or typo visitors

• Can bring targeted traffic developed domains

Cons

• Domains with PPC parking pages on them can drop out of the search engine indexes.

Prior Development

Is there any proof of existing traffic?

A domain name with a steady stream of traffic is generally considered a good domain name. Regardless of the method in which you intend to make money as a domainer, the issue of verifiable traffic will always be a major factor in determining a domain name's value or its effectiveness at generating traffic that can be monetized in some way. If a domain seller is claiming existing traffic ask to see reliable statistics reports.

Is the domain indexed by search engines?

Even if you park a domain with a PPC landing page provider, existing search engine indexing is likely to keep traffic coming through a domain for at least a little while. Check on the number of pages indexed by the major search engines: Google, Yahoo and Bing.

Does the domain have existing backlinks?

Backlinks allows you to send traffic directly from other websites to your domain, so as a general rule the more backlinks you have the more traffic you'll get.

What is the quality of the backlinks?

Some backlinks offer more benefit than others. Backlinks from quality sites that are related to your domain's subject matter are more likely to send traffic that will translate into revenue. Backlinks from low quality sites that send uninterested visitors may help your traffic stats but add nothing to your revenue.

Does the domain have any PageRank?

Google PageRank is a number between 0 and 9 that is allocated to a domain as a measurement of the number and quality of backlinks it has. The more backlinks a domain has and the higher the quality of those links, the higher the resulting PageRank. Lower rankings of 1 to 2 are relatively easy to attain, but rankings of 3 to 4 indicate that there is a healthy amount of quality traffic that is likely to come from existing backlinks. Ranks of 5 and above are not common and represent a significant chance of very high levels of traffic.

Prior Development: Research methods

Alexa

Alexa (alexa.com) is a publicly accessible service that can tell you how much traffic a domain has and can also provide comparisons to other domains. Each site that Alexa has statistics on is given a ranking where the smaller the number, the higher the rank. If a domain has had a significant level of traffic you will be able to view its traffic history through Alexa, however for low traffic domains available information may be limited. If you are considering purchasing any domain that requires a significant investment it is reasonable to expect it to have a healthy Alexa rank. The results of Web site traffic appear on a graph, where you can also view the "reach" of the site, its ranking, and the percentage of pages that are viewed on a daily basis over several months' time. You can also compare other sites' traffic by typing the name of other sites in the text boxes and clicking "Compare Sites".

Compete.com

Compete.com is service that can provide very comprehensive statistics on almost every active domain on the internet. Information can be accessed on a domain's number of unique visitors, overall visits, page views, average stay time, as well as age, gender and income demographics. Some of this information, such as unique visitors, is available free of charge. Others information, such as page views, is accessible through a Pro membership.

Archive.org

The archive.org website provides the "WayBack Machine" feature, which allows you to review historical data relating to the activity of a domain you are considering during the time it was registered.

Browser plugins

Some of the fastest and easiest research tools to use are extensions that plug directly into your web browser. For example, if you use the Google Chrome web browser you can utilize the "Chrome SEO" extension tool to simply go to a domain and click the "Chrome SEO" button in your toolbar. A small window will appear at the top right of your screen that displays all of the key information you need to assess prior traffic development on a domain.

Internet Explorer is not equipped with plugin functionality, but Mozilla Firefox users can find a number of useful SEO tools by doing a general web search for them.

Industry factors

How much demand is there within the related industries?

You can only know how much traffic you can draw that relates to a given industry when you know how much demand there is for products and services within it. The easiest way to check this is to refer again to the Google Adwords Keyword Planner tool we used earlier. As well as the data we have already covered, this tool also gives you an estimate of how many people are searching for a given keyword each month.

Once you have identified the industry related keywords for the domain, simply check on the number of searches per month for those keywords. The tool can provide both global search volumes as well as local search volumes for specific countries.

How strong is competition within the related industries?

Often the industries that enjoy the most demand also must contend with the highest level of competition. The easiest way to find out how many other domains are competing for the traffic in your target industry is to search for your industry related keyphrases in Google and see how many results appear. The number of results is your approximate number of competitors. For example, if your niche is raising chicken, the search for "chicken pens" yields over 1.5 million results, which is very high competition for a keyword with a global average monthly search volume of only 2,900. However the keyword "chicken waterer" returns 39,000 against a global search volume of 4,400 at the time of writing this book. Try to find domain names that have the best possible balance of high demand and low competition.

Domain factors - Type in traffic

How much deliberate type in traffic can the domain draw?

There are a few key factors that determine whether a domain is likely to receive type-in traffic. There is no strict measurement method for these attributes, so you will be best served to exercise your own judgment in consideration of the following factors.

Trending

Commonly used words or phrases can form very effective type-in domain names. Many common words or phrases are already registered, however new trends are continually evolving that deliver us with new words, phrases and terminology. This presents an opportunity for astute domainers who stay abreast of current events and trends to snap up new type-in domains as they become socially relevant.

Industry Correlation

Direct correlation of a domain with a particular industry can also lead to high traffic type-in domains. Earlier we discussed the domains "netbooks.com" and "creditcards.com". Both of these are excellent examples of creating a domain that correlates with a specific industry. Again, most domains that match existing industries are already registered so the key is to look for emerging industries and jump on the related domains before anyone else can get to them.

Easy to remember

The domain name should be short and easy to remember, which will increase the chances of people actually being able to type the address into their browser when they choose to. As a general rule, the shorter a domain is the easier it is to remember.

Easy to say

If the domain name is difficult for people to say or correctly pronounce, don't use it! Difficult to say translates to difficult to type. Also, be aware of homonyms. Homonyms are words that are pronounced the same but have different meanings, for example plane and plain. This can cause confusion and divert your traffic to someone else's domain however it works both ways and can also allow you to capitalize on someone else's type-in traffic.

Easy to spell

It is critical for people to easily be able to remember the exact spelling of your domain name. If people can't remember how the domain name is spelled they can't type it into their address bar. Stick with relatively simple and easily spelled words.

No punctuation

Hyphens, periods, numbers and so on only add complexity to a domain name, making it harder to remember. Studies have shown that domain names with hyphens or other special characters are much more difficult for people to remember. If the only domain name you can find for a certain set of keywords has punctuation in it, try to find an alternative set of keywords to work with instead.

Extension type

The .com extension has always been considered the most valuable because of its global popularity and branding. People have become accustomed to thinking of "dot com" when trying to remember the domain name of a site they want to visit. While .net, .info and others are making some headway in popularity, the .com extension is still most likely to be the first one that people will try.

How much accidental type in traffic can the domain draw?

Keyword typos

The sections above regarding trending and industry correlation can also apply to assessing the potential for keyword typos. We used the example of "creditcards.com" as a domain likely to receive type in traffic because of the keywords it contains.

At the same time, an accidentally mistyped version of this domain can also receive traffic, for example "creditvards.com". Note that in this example the second "c" in the domain has been replaced by the letter that sits next to it on the keyboard, the letter "v".

Misspelling typos

Sometimes domains are typed incorrectly through accidentally hitting the wrong letter on the keyboard. However sometimes they can also be typed incorrectly through a person not being aware of how to spell a particular word. For example, "netbooks.com" might be miss-spelled as "nettbooks.com".

DON'T acquire trademark typos

Whether you are aiming to acquire keyword or miss-spelled typo domains, do not make the mistake of registering or purchasing anything remotely related to a trademark. For example, don't touch "ebaye.com" with a ten foot barge pole. If you own a domain that infringes trademark in any way you have a good chance of facing a lawsuit. Stick strictly to generic and industry related keywords instead.

Domain factors – Search engine friendliness

Domain keywords

If a domain is comprised of an exact keyphrase it has a much improved chance of ranking high in the SERPS for that phrase. For example, "creditcards.com" is first in the overall rankings for the search "credit cards", second only to Google's own related news results. It even outranks all of the credit card companies. You can be sure it would not have achieved the same feat if not for the key words comprising the domain name. Note that this principle really only applies of you get the exact keywords searched for in the correct order, without punctuation, and with a ".com" extension. You may still be effective with a ".net" or ".org" extension, but only one of these two others, and only if the ".com" extension is not already ranking well.

Extension type

As just mentioned, despite rigorous debate results do tend to demonstrate that search engines give preference to ".com" extensions in their results. Typically, if you had a ".com", ".net" and ".org" domain all using the exact same wording, they would rank in the exact order I just listed them in. It is possible for other extensions to rank, but again this is usually only if there is little active competition. Always make your top four extension preferences ".com", ".net", ".org" and ".co", in that order and only consider other extensions if there is rock solid proof of existing traffic.

No Punctuation

As with the less preferable domain extensions, it is possible for domains including punctuation to draw search engine traffic, but not without a great deal of SEO effort. Where a domain like "creditcards.com" can draw search engine traffic almost effortlessly, a domain along the lines of "credit-cards-central.com" will have a much harder time. As much as possible, invest only in domains with no punctuation unless you have absolute proof of traffic and revenue the domain has already generated.

Overall traffic potential

A precise estimation of traffic potential is not really possible given the number of factors involved in its assessment. Nor is it advisable that you try to arrive at a precise estimate of X number of visitors per day, as such a calculation would require excessive amounts of time. Rather, what you should do is run through the list of qualities described above for each domain you consider and make an approximate assessment of what you believe the traffic potential to be. General labels such as "high potential", "average potential" and "low potential" will be enough to help you make investment decisions.

You will need to weigh each of these aspects against each other, as often it will not be possible to put a tick in every box on your list of ideal domain characteristics. For example, a domain may be difficult to spell, which might be because it is actually a great typo domain to own. Make each assessment on a case by case basis and try to find the best balance of attributes you can.

Domain Valuation: Assessing Overall Value

Once you have completed your assessment of revenue potential and traffic potential you are ready to form an overall picture of the value of the domain. Remember our earlier method of determining value was:

• The average revenue per visitor multiplied by the number of visitors

Once you have taken the appropriate steps to evaluating traffic and revenue potential for a domain, remember to come back to this key principle. Here is a rough guide to how to classify your results:

• Strong revenue potential X strong traffic potential = high quality prospect
• Strong revenue potential X weak traffic potential = mid quality prospect

- Weak revenue potential X strong traffic potential = low quality prospect
- Weak revenue potential X weak traffic potential = nil quality prospect

Again, this is a rough guide to classifying potential investments and you should bear in mind that nothing is ever set in stone. You will find you are often surprised by results that turn out to be highly different from what you projected. The main purpose of this process is to avoid the worst domain names that become liabilities instead of assets. As you gain more experience you will become increasingly proficient in evaluating prospects. In the meantime, use the information that we have just finished discussing to get you started on the right foot.

Domain Acquisition: Creating Domains

Choosing a Registrar

Over the past several years, the number of registrars has increased dramatically and the ensuing competition has caused prices to remain very reasonable. Because there are so many registrars to choose from, each with their own unique pricing, added features and tools, you must be sure to conduct sufficient research when selecting the one you will use. This may take some time.

Obviously, you will want to deal with the best registrar for your specific needs and priorities, taking into consideration price, administrative support, security, transfer policies, and so on. While the majority of registrars have solid reputations, some do not and it is very important that you discover which of them ought to be avoided.

The best way to do this is to register, typically free of charge, at several domaining forums and read the feedback posted by more experienced domainers. Most forums have a registrar feedback section that allows domainers to elaborate on their most recent dealings with various registrars. Reading these kinds of sections is a superb way to get the current state on registrars you are considering and you will be able to quickly ascertain those who have superb reputations and those who do not. Like many businesses, the level of customer service, responsiveness and infrastructure from registrars does seem to go through periods of fluctuation. The domain related forums will enable you to rapidly assess which registrars are providing a high level of service right now and which are currently to be avoided.

Some of the major criteria you should use to evaluate a registrar are:

Price: We all want to save money, but you'd be wise to take your time and fully evaluate several of the major registrars, even if their prices vary greatly. Very low prices are typically (but not always) associated with reduced support or fewer options and are usually designed to "get you in the door" so the registrar can attempt to sell you additionally products and services. Make sure you get a complete picture of what a registrars pricing model provides you.

Security: You are probably wondering why security is an issue with registrars. Allow me to be the person to inform you that there have been numerous instances in which a domain name has been "stolen" from its rightful owner by a clever thief who manages to assume the owners identity and divert control of the domain name. Check on the history and feedback regarding the level of security provided.

Administrative Support: Registering a domain name will require some degree of ongoing administration on your part and you should research which registrars have solid reputations for administrative support. It is well known that some registrars are notorious for being very slow to respond to customer e-mails or phone calls and you certainly would want to avoid them. Look for registrars who have recent reports of fast and quality customer support.

The Appendix section contains a list of the major domain name registrars. You should note that these companies frequently change their prices, service offerings, etc. When it comes to buying domain names, it is best to shop around and see if there are any sales or other incentives being offered. This is common and you can often get some great deals!

Getting started

In the previous sections you were given some pointers on the characteristics of effective and valuable domain names. Keeping these pointers in mind, it's time to discuss creating a domain name. There are several resources available to help you in creative process of coming up with domain names. Some resources are as simple as a piece of paper, pencil, and your own creativity, while others are more sophisticated, such as online tools. You can use any of these resources or a combination of several resources. Explore them all and find out what works for you.

Getting ideas

Brain dump

Out of all of your resources, this is the least sophisticated but a good place to start. Chances are that you already have some ideas. All that is required is a place to record your ideas and a cup of coffee (or whatever gets your creative drive going). Type or write down all the ideas that come to you. Then use some of the other resources listed below to help expand your ideas and come up with synonyms and word associations.

Thesaurus

Dust off your thesaurus, use a word processing thesaurus (such as MS Word), or go to an online thesaurus, such as thesaurus.reference.com and enter some of the keywords you've come up with. Then, record any additional words that appeal to you.

Current events

Keep abreast of current events using any and all available mediums, such as newspapers, magazines, TV and movies. Trends and hot topics are forever changing. Even commercials can generate ideas for good domain names. All you have to do is tune in and when something appeals to you, record it. You'd be surprised at the ideas that you can get from the news and media.

Google Product Search

Go to the Google Product Search (google.com/shopping) page and simply keep refreshing the screen, every reload will display a fresh new list of products people have found using the search only moments ago. This gives you up to the minute data on what people are spending money on and the exact keywords they are using to help them find what they want to buy.

Keyword search tools

There are some good keyword search tools you can use on the Internet to help in your quest for domain names. Some tools are free, such as those listed below. However, others you have to pay to use. You can find additional keyword search tools simply by using one of the search engines on the Internet, such as Yahoo! or Google.

Adwords Keyword Planner (AKP)

https://adwords.google.com/ko/KeywordPlanner/Home

The new Adwords tool that included Adwords Keyword Tool and Traffic Estimator. It fully replaced the old Adworkds Keyword Tool.

Insights for Search

http://google.com/insights/search

Analyzes and compares search patterns across specific regions, categories, and time frames. You can then use this information to anticipate search volume based on search behavior, for example, during a specific time of year.

Google Trends

http://www.google.com/trends/

Google Trends displays what people have been recently searching for with Google. It currently includes the Hot Searches and the new Top Charts feature, which displays the data in graphical format.

WordTracker (WT)

http://freekeywords.wordtracker.com

WordTracker helps you identify keywords and phrases related to your domain and determine how popular they are. In addition, you can determine what other sites also use these keywords and phrases.

Keyword Eye

http://www.keywordeye.com/

Keyword Eye is an easy to use visual keyword tool that has a free version with allows you to search up to 10 keywords a day and gives you access to 100 keywords per report. It is mostly suited for high level ideas to get started with.

Keyword Spy

http://www.keywordspy.com/

Keyword Spy has a set of very useful tools including a free tool called Domain Spy that make searching for domain information extremely easy. You can get pretty accurate results about a site in terms of their PPC spending, the main keywords they are bidding on and their main competitors in the business – paid and organic.

SemRush

http://www.semrush.com/

SemRush is another paid tool that offers a very useful free version that gives interesting information about the keyword chosen, such as the number of results for the keyword along with a featured called "related keyword", allowing you to find additional ideas to search for in your quest for a good domain.

sTypo

sTypo (stypo.com) is a search tool of a different sort. It searches for typographical misspellings in domain names and then runs the name through the Overture Search Tool to see if it is available. Unlike some of the other tools, this one is not free. The cost is about $50. However, you may get your money back and then some if you find some lucrative domain names.

Whois?

Whois? (whois.com) allows you to perform lookups to see if a domain name is available, or you can search for existing domains to purchase. If applicable, you can also see which domains are up for auction and where a domain is in the sales process. The nice thing about this site is that you have the choice of specifying which of these options you want to make use of.

Domain Acquisition: Buying Existing Domains

Thus far you have learned how to identify a high-quality domain name, how to create your own name, how to search and qualify the name using a variety of tools, and how to register your domain name. The hard part is over. So, let's move on to explore other areas of domaining, such as ways you can obtain existing domain names. Here are a few ways to do this:

- Finding and buying an expired name
- Participating in an auction
- Purchasing domains from aftermarket resellers
- Purchasing from a third party

Finding and Buying an Expired Domain

Over 20,000 domain names expire each day. Domains expire for various reasons, ranging from an owner simply forgetting to renew the registration to those who have simply lost interest in the domain and have decided to let the registration lapse. While the vast majority of expiring domain names may be of little value, some are actually quite valuable and as you would expect, the competition for them is fierce.

A large number of domainers specialize in the identification and buying of expired domain names, or "drop catching" as the practice is known. Many of those who specialize in drop catching are looking for domain names with existing traffic that they can in some way monetize. Others are looking for names they believe they can sell to others. Whatever their reason for becoming involved in the buying of expired domain names, domainers who engage in this practice approach it with a passion that is obvious when you speak with them.

The drop catching arena is very fast paced and complex, and is not a place where rookies historically do well. While drop catching may seem to be a simple concept, there is nothing simple about becoming an effective drop catcher. Statistics show that many domain names are registered by a new owner within minutes of them expiring and becoming available for purchase. With automated tools the registration is often done in seconds. You are going to have to do a good bit of studying before you become proficient at this fascinating aspect of domaining. This is assuming, of course, that you aspire to a level of proficiency that will enable you to compete with serious drop catchers who are pursuing the same expired domain names as you.

Every domain name has an expiration date. When an expiration date passes without the registration being renewed, the domain name enters what is called the On Hold or Registrar-Hold phase which lasts from 30-45 days. If the domain name registration is not renewed during this time it enters the Redemption phase, which lasts 30 days. If the registration is not renewed during this phase, it enters the Pending Delete phase, which lasts five days. At the end of the fifth day, the domain name becomes available for purchase.

The expiration dates for specific domain names can be found by looking up the domain name record. This can be done using the "whois" search function at VeriSign. The results of the "whois" search will provide the owner's contact information, the domain name's creation and expiration dates, current status, and technical information associated with the domain name.

Serious drop catchers use detailed lists of expired domain names to assist them. There are also special tools you can use (some are free, some must be purchased) to locate and categorize the many thousands of expiring or recently expired domain names. The domain name industry has given birth to several associated business niches and it was only a matter of time before someone figured out a way of making money by helping people buy expired domain names. As a result, there are now numerous commercial drop catching services that, for a fee, will provide current lists of expiring domain names and other services that greatly increase your chances of obtaining the domain names you desire.

It is important that you understand how competitive the drop catching game is. Most serious drop catchers utilize a variety of commercial services and automated tools to locate and buy dropped domain names. All else being equal, their knowledge and use of technology will beat your inexperience and manual processes every time. Therefore, if you desire to become proficient at buying expired domain names, you should embrace the methods used by serious drop catchers from the start of your domaining career.

DomainsBot.com

I believe DomainsBot (domainsbot.com) is one of the best tool on the market for finding expired domain names. You simply type in a domain name or a keyword you're interested in and you are immediately presented with all the domains that are available (also premium domains) that you can grab right now.

Refer to the list below for some good sites to help you search for expired domains.

- www.justdropped.com
- www.Enom.com
- www.pool.com
- www.domainpond.com
- www.snapcheck.com
- www.snapcheck.com
- www.dotster.com
- www.registercompass.org
- www.whois-search.com
- www.expireddomains.net

Participating in Domain Name Auctions

Auctions for domain names are essentially no different than any other type of auction. You can bid on domain names, just as you would in any other kind of auction. The sites listed below are well-known auction sites:

- www.afternic.com
- www.pool.com
- www.moniker.com
- www.snapnames.com
- https://auctions.godaddy.com
- www.sedo.com
- www.namejet.com
- www.flippa.com

Be aware that when you bid on a name, the site actually places the bid for you. Much like eBay, once a bid is placed, the auction site determines a bid expiration, compares all bids, and then notifies the winner.

Purchasing Domains from Aftermarket Resellers

Aftermarket resellers are those who sell domain names that were previously registered through websites that deal specifically in buying and selling domains. These websites post the domains that are for sale on behalf of the domain owner, but for a fee. Through these Web sites, you can view the domain names that are for sale and make purchases as well. Once the purchase is made, the domain is transferred to the new owner. In order to place a bid through any reseller site you must become a member. Membership is usually free.

Pricing

Aftermarket sales can be a bit steep because sellers are well aware of how important domain names are to the success of a business. An average aftermarket domain can cost $100 or more. There are even some that range from thousands to hundreds of thousands of dollars.

Appraisals

So, how do you go about determining if a domain is worth paying out the big bucks? Like real estate appraisers, there are appraisal services available (for a fee of course) to establish the value of a domain name. They use algorithms to determine the value. For example, one word .com domains, two and three character domains, high traffic keywords, and brand-specific names are worth a lot more than the others. Sellers usually also have their domain appraised, so you can ask to see the appraisal.

Flat Rates vs. Auctions

Depending on the purchasing method offered by aftermarket domain sellers, you can either pay a flat rate or participate in an auction. Some aftermarket domains offer a combination of both methods, such as AfterNIC (the aftermarket sales leader). Flat rates are just that – what you must pay to purchase the domain. With the auctions on the other hand, the seller sets a minimum bid amount and buyers can then place their bids. You do have the option of foregoing the bidding process and paying asking price to secure your purchase. However, be prepared for it to be costly.

Payments

The safest way of paying for your aftermarket domain is using an escrow, or a secure, third-party service. Most sites that buy and sell domains offer an escrow service.

Under New Management

Know what you are getting into when you purchase an aftermarket domain. Some sites may have a good or bad reputation. Therefore, as the new owner, you could either benefit from the existing reputation or find that you need to take steps to improve the perception of the domain.

Aftermarket Domains

There are some good sites that specialize in aftermarket sales. Refer to the list below to get started:

- www.afternic.com
- www.sedo.com
- www.tdnam.com
- www.buydomains.com
- https://auctions.godaddy.com
- www.greatdomains.com

Buying a Domain Name from a Third Party

Every domainer will invariably find a domain name they wish to add to their portfolio that is already owned by someone else. Assuming the he or she is willing to fork over the cash for such a domain, the question is whether or not the owner is willing to sell it.

Before you approach the owner of the domain name, you must make a few decisions.

- How profitable will owning the domain name be?
- How much are you willing to pay for it?
- Are you in a hurry to take ownership?

- Are you going to contact the owner or will you utilize a middleman?

Buying a domain name from a third party can be tricky because in many cases you are dealing with someone who is not conversant in the ways of the domain name industry. You may have to educate the person regarding what you are trying to do and how you suggest doing it. Many owners are somewhat surprised when they receive an inquiry regarding a domain name they own, especially if they registered it long ago, never used it and forgot about it.

No matter the situation, your demeanor and approach with the domain owner has a direct impact on how smoothly the transaction is executed or if it is executed at all. There are known cases of owners becoming irritated or insulted by buyers with less than adequate negotiating skills, who have then not only refused to sell the domain name but have renewed its registration for several more years and sat on it out of spite! Tread softly with owners of domain names you want to buy.

Before you contact a domain owner to inquire about purchasing their domain name, follow the tips listed below to ensure your anonymity. Should the domain owner research you to find out who they are selling to and potentially find out you are well known in the domaining world, they are most likely going to charge you more.

- Set up an e-mail account from which to inquire and negotiate domain name purchases.
- Do not reveal your entire name in your new e-mail account.
- When you sign your e-mail messages, do not include your last name.

Finding Domain Owners

The easiest way to find the contact information for a domain owner is to use www.whois.net. Refer to the earlier description of how to use the Whois domain lookup.

Approaching a Domain Owner

There are several ways to approach the owner of a domain name you want to buy. You have to decide which approach you want to use and what you will do if that approach does not yield the desired results. A few of the more common approaches are listed below.

- Via email

- Through domain forums and/or newsgroups
- Through internet merchants

E-mail Inquiries

The simplest way to approach the owner is to send him a short, concise e-mail message that gets right to the heart of the matter.

Some domainers think it best not to mention that you want to buy the domain name, rather they prefer to ask the owner if he has any intentions of using it. Others, including me, believe that it's best to get the issue on the table right from the start. You will have to decide which method is best for each specific situation.

The owner may not respond to your first e-mail message, thinking it to be SPAM clogging his or her inbox. If you do not hear from them within three working days try sending a follow up e-mail message. Be sure to edit the message so that it is clear that it is the second of two messages you have sent.

The owner may respond and indicate an interest in selling the domain name. If he or she states an inflated price, send a reply indicating saying "I was thinking of making an offer more in the xxx to xxx range." Their reply to your response will give you an idea whether you have realistic chances at buying the domain name.

Lowball Offer

If a domain owner responds to your inquiry indicating that he or she is interested in selling, but does not mention a price, you should respond with a "lowball" offer. In many cases, the owner wants to unload the domain name and will be willing to sell it for a very low price.

Finalizing the Sale

Once you and the owner have settled on a price, you should send him or her a summary e-mail message listing the price and other relevant details associated with the transaction. Ask him or her to reply confirming his or her agreement with all conditions of the transaction.

It is highly recommended that you seek the services of an attorney if the domain sale is over $10,000. Large transactions have been known to experience friction on occasion. It is best to spend the money to ensure that the sale is conducted in a legally defendable manner.

Executing the Sale

You must decide how the payment will be handled (cashier's check, PayPal, Escrow service, etc.) and what the date and time of the transaction will be. Once the money is transferred, you may initiate the transfer of the domain name to you by contacting the registrar holding the domain name and completing the process stated by the registrar's representative.

Forums and Message Boards

There are online organizations, such as forums and message boards that cater to domainers and are a good place to look for domain names that are for sale. In order to inquire about a domain though, you have to subscribe to that forum, however registration is usually free. Below are some forums to look into.

- www.namepros.com
- www.domainstate.com
- www.domainnameforum.com
- www.dnforum.com
- www.cctlds.com

For a full list of domainer forums check the Appendix section.

Internet Merchants

Internet merchants, such as eBay, provide an arena for buying domain names. You might not think that eBay is a good place to buy or sell domain names, but it routinely has thousands of domain names for sale. The sales process works the same as anything else you can buy from eBay – through an auction.

Revenue During Ownership: PPC Parking

In the previous sections you learned that parking a domain name generates revenue when people visit your domain name and click on one of the PPC advertisements they are presented with. You basically have two choices when it comes to creating a landing page: you can create and operate it yourself or you can outsource the task to one of several companies that offer parking services. These PPC companies, often referred to as aggregators, create landing pages containing advertisements that are relevant to the specific domain name.

In other words, if the domain name you are parking is related to shoes, the parking service creates a landing page that contains ads focusing on shoe merchants. The various shoe merchants have already agreed to compensate internet search firms like Google or Yahoo for traffic it sends to their websites. When they pay Google for this traffic, Google shares a portion of this money with the PPC Company who created and operates the landing page. The PPC Company subsequently pays a portion of its share to the owner of the domain name.

Allowing a parking service to create and operate your landing page will enable you to quickly get your domain name generating revenue. This is especially true if you are a beginner with little knowledge of domaining and / or if you are not capable of developing your own landing pages. It takes a good bit of training and practice to become fully competent at creating effective landing pages. Many domainers choose to focus their efforts toward the identification and acquisition of good domain names rather than becoming a "techie."

Ultimately, you will have to decide what best suits your personal goals as a domainer. I strongly recommend that beginners, especially those without a background in web design and related web skills, partner with a reputable PPC company. For most this is the shortest path to actually getting your domain name into the online revenue generating arena.

When utilizing the PPC parking method of making money from domain names, it is important to remember that the most money is made from domain names that already have traffic coming to them. The PPC Company you use will do its best to monetize the existing traffic and maximize the revenue-generating capability of your domain name. Because it takes a portion of the revenue generated by the parked name, the PPC Company is highly motivated to make your landing page the best it can possibly be.

Once you have decided that you are going to partner with a PPC company, you should do a significant amount of research on the various companies offering parking services. As in any industry, there are differences among these companies that make some of them more desirable as a partner than others. Some offer different payment plans or have entry requirements that are stricter than others.

It is strongly suggested that you go to several of the more popular domainers' Web forums and ask for input and advice. Most of these forums have sections dedicated to the topic of PPC companies and I believe reading and asking for people's opinions is the best way to obtain a balanced view of a PPC company's reputation and current operating procedures. Domain name parking is one facet of the domain name industry that is constantly evolving and you must continuously study it to remain current and ensure you are partnering with the PPC Company that will result in the highest return on your investment.

When you select a PPC company as your partner you will be given instructions on how to associate your domain name with their parking service. These instructions must be followed to the last detail or you may find you spend a good amount of time trying to figure out why you are not making any money from your domain name! Most PPC companies have dedicated support functions that can assist you during the "linking" process. This support is one of the most important features a PPC company can offer and you should do everything you can to determine which company will perform best for you in this regard.

Some domainers add a For Sale sign on their landing pages. The PPC page enables them to prove the domain name is capable of generating revenue, which in turn makes it an attractive prospect to potential buyers. Some PPC companies do not allow this practice, so be sure to check with yours should you decide to use this tactic.

PPC Parking Bottom Line

So just how much can you make from PPC? If you collect the right portfolio of domains each with significant amounts of traffic you could have a regular source of income solely from PPC landing pages. In the world of domaining, this is known as a "buy and hold" strategy, which is a term borrowed from general investment circles. This concept is based on the view that holding onto an asset over a long period of time will allow for any fluctuations in income levels to average out and result in an overall profit.

Below are some examples of parked domain names. Notice they are all misspellings of real sites. These sites are not even websites because they go directly to the landing page when a visitor types the name in to their browser. Typo domains can be a gold mine and if you can manage to secure them and generic names, i.e. domains deliberately typed in, have even greater revenue potential.

- www.loneofficers.com
- www.mental-illness.com
- www.franklincovery.com

Choosing an Aggregator

The list below contains a list of some well-known sites that provide aggregator services along with a brief description of each and their payment thresholds. There is usually no charge to register with them, but the payout restrictions vary. You can also visit www.ppcincome.com for more information.

- www.sedo.com
- www.fabulous.com
- www.domainsponsor.com

Be sure you understand the PPC Company's minimum payout policy. Normally, a $20 monthly payout minimum means that you must accumulate at least $20 in ad clicks per month, or the balance is carried forward to the next month. However, payment agreements vary from company to company so be sure to read the fine print.

Tips and Tricks for PPC Parking

Previous sections outlined the key attributes of valuable domain names. You may find in your quest for names that many of the best names are already taken, but do not give up! There are

110

plenty of methods for finding great domain names, such as registering variations of misspelled popular domain names.

A "typo" of someone else's domain name could lead to profit for you. Each day millions of people type in misspelled words while attempting to search on the Web. You can take advantage of this by registering a popular domain name, with one twist - the name is spelled wrong or some of the letters are transposed. For example, you could register a variation of shoes.com, such as "shose.com" or "sheos.com". Do not expect to receive the capacity of visitors that you would on such a popular site, but you would have a very good chance of receiving at least some visitors.

You can also access the following Web sites to assist with researching the most commonly misspelled words:

- http://www.wsu.edu/~brians/errors/misspelled.html
- http://www.yourdictionary.com/library/misspelled.html

Parking Services

Something else you should consider before purchasing a domain is finding a good parking service, which provides a place for you to register and maintain your domain if it is not part of or not ready to be a Web site. Some parking services to consider are below. For a full list check the Appendix.

- www.Sedo.com
- www.Fabulous.com
- www.Afternic.com
- www.Bodis.com

Revenue During Ownership: Affiliate Programs

We discussed earlier how the two primary means of generating revenue from domains are PPC and affiliate programs. We have also covered how a PPC Company takes care of the creation and management of landing pages for you. In order for revenue generation from affiliate programs to be able to stack up as an option against PPC landing pages you will need to find landing page creation methods that are as fast and painless as possible. You will only select a few high potential domains to actually put development time into, so if you want to earn from affiliate programs for the rest you will need to know some shortcuts. Some tools and services that will let you create affiliate landing pages almost instantly are as follows.

iMODO

iMODO (iModo.c om) bills itself as a domain parking service that generates websites with automatically updating content and social networking integration. Domainers can park their entire portfolio and simply specify the keywords that the associated sites should be based on. iMODO generated sites can include links, news, photos, video, product listings, directories and forums. You also have the option of including a "For Sale" sign on your landing page and have your domain added to iMODO's catalogue of available domains. Additionally, the staff will help you to negotiate a sale if you require. Affiliate revenue payouts are on a net 45 basis with a threshold of $25. Access to iMODO is completely free of charge but you must have at least 25 quality domains in order to qualify for access.

Developing Domains

Certain domains have an amount of potential that just cannot be fully realized through basic landing pages like those described in the previous two chapters. If you have a domain that you have tested through one of the PPC or Affiliate landing page services discussed above and found that it is performing extremely well, you might find that having a custom website developed for the domain can multiply your revenue even further. However, the decision to invest more time and money into such a domain shouldn't stop you from trying to find the best balance of efficiency and effectiveness available to you. The services that follow understand the goals of domainers, so when you come to developing a domain in your portfolio consider one of these operators first.

Minisites.com

Minisites.com is a website development service that caters specifically to the needs of domainers. They also have hard proof of sites they've created doing very well in the search engine rankings (see the image to the left). They offer three different minisite creation packages, each with its own pricing menu, and every site includes:

- Dedicated Project Manager
- Unique Content Written by Native English Speakers
- Custom Text Logo Design
- Attractive Graphic Header Design
- Linkbuilding Campaign
- Flexible Monetization Options
- Targeted Keyword Research
- Search Engine Optimization
- Ability to Add Your Own Content Post-Launch
- Free Hosting and Email Forwarding Accounts

In addition to hiring them to create your minisite you can also subscribe to their content creation service and have fresh original articles added to your site on a regular basis. This keeps both people and search engines coming back regularly to see what's new, so if your domain shows exceptional promise this service can be well worth your while.

dDevelop

dDevelop (dDevelop.com) is a web development service run by Daniel Sanchez who understands exactly what domainers are trying to achieve, because he is a domainer himself. It is through his own hands on experience of developing quality domains that he has learned what does and does not make for an effective minisite. He offers flexibility in the features your minisite can incorporate, with prices ranging from around $195 to $250.

Domain Mass Development

Once you have proven to yourself that you know how to pick which of your domains are going to become more profitable through development, you can consider having multiple domains developed at once to save time and money. Domain Mass Development (domainmassdevelopment.com) is a service designed specifically to allow you to efficiently develop multiple domains, with prices starting from $999 for 20 domains. Packages include a dedicated project manager, turnaround time of 7 – 10 days, creation of original content and monetization of sites. At only $49.95 or less for each domain this makes for an extremely competitive service, once you know how to choose the right domains to develop.

Selling Domains

Thus far, you have learned how and where to buy domain names and how to generate revenue from them. Now, let's explore the side of domaining where you have the potential to get the biggest payoff - selling domain names. Selling a domain name can be broken down into three distinct phases:

- Establishing the market value
- Establishing your minimum sale price
- Selecting a sales strategy

Establishing the Market Value

In order to make as much of a profit as possible from a sale you must establish what a domain name's market value is. This is easier said than done because many domain names have unique qualities and characteristics that don't lend themselves well to standard valuation calculators. A common saying in the domaining business is, "A domain name is worth whatever someone is willing to pay for it."

One of the most effective ways to establish the market value of a domain name is to get an appraisal. There are services that will conduct an appraisal for a fee. This method can be accurate as long as you are dealing with an established vendor who has an excellent track record. Some domainers feel the best way to get an appraisal is to simply ask other domainers for their opinions. This is easily done through various domain related forums and is a method I strongly encourage you to consider.

Establishing Your Minimum Sale Price

You cannot move forward in the selling process without knowing what your absolute minimum sale price is. It is to be expected that potential buyers will try to negotiate a lower price than what you are asking and you must establish a baseline price you will not go below. Establishing your minimum price enables you to properly plan a series of offer & counter offer scenarios that in turn enable you to negotiate from a position of strength.

There are some people in the domain business that prefer using a mathematical way of determining the base value and thus the sale price of a domain: monthly revenue x 12 = annual rate. Let's say that on average, you make $40 per month on a domain. Multiply $40 by 12 to get an estimate for what your yearly income is for that domain, which is $480. You can then take it a step further and project to a potential buyer a 2-year profit of $960.

If you'd rather get some help in determining the sale price of your domain, there are services out there that can evaluate your domain and provide you with a document stating the net worth of your domain. You do have to pay for this service. However, it may carry more weight when it comes time to negotiate a sale price with a potential buyer. Below are some of the free and commercial sites you can use for such services.

- www.domainappraisal.org
- www.networksolutions.com
- www.valuate.com
- www.estibot.com
- www.domainindex.com

Each appraiser has their own way of determining the value of your domain. There is no industry standard formula. Therefore, the value you are quoted may differ from one appraiser to another. A poll is sometimes run to ask users their take on the domain, which adds real world evidence to an evaluation of what someone might be willing to pay for the domain.

Selecting a Sales Strategy

There are various resources you can utilize to sell your domain name. The major resources are listed below, followed by descriptions of each, and recommended references.

- Domain agencies and aftermarket brokers
- Auctions
- Direct with potential buyers
- eBay
- Domain-related forums

Domain Agencies and Aftermarket Brokers

By selling your domain through an agency or aftermarket broker you can turn over all the legwork to them. This can come in handy when you have several domains to sell. All you need to do is provide the price you want for your domains and they do all the rest. However they do come at a price, though usually a minimal one.

Once option you have when you use a broker is using private placement, which means that you have your broker list your domain name without listing all the details. This option eliminates the need to regularly check Wanted and other listings. Below are lists of recommended agencies and aftermarket brokers.

Agencies
- www.dotcomagency.com
- www.idomainbrokers.com
- www.erealestate.com

Aftermarket Brokers
- www.buydomains.com
- www.sedo.com
- www.afternic.com
- www.domainagency.com

Check out the Appendix section for additional agencies and brokers.

Auctions

Participating in auctions was discussed earlier, but from a buying standpoint. You can also use auctions to sell your domain. The concept is the same – you put your domain up for sale on the auction and others make bids on it. An advantage to selling via an auction is that the process moves quickly and you can close a sale quicker than some of the other selling options. However, you sometimes end up getting less for your domain due to the quick turn-around.

Auction sites you can use are listed in the "Participating in Domain Name Auctions" section.

Advertising

There are sites out there that you can use to advertise your domain sale, such as Google Base for example. All you have to do is provide the information on the sale of your domain and post it. You can also use Whois.com. If you are a member you can create a "For Sale" sign for your domain via your member profile. You can find all the details on putting a domain up for sale on the Whois.com site.

If you decide to put your name up for sale on any site, always make sure you include the words "for sale", your contact information (including your e-mail address), your domain name and the sale price.

eBay

Using eBay to buy domain names was discussed earlier and can also be used to post a domain for sale on a bidding basis. However, eBay also offers a "Buy it Now" function so you can list your domain for a set price instead of through an auction route.

Domaining Related Forums

Some of the most popular and well-known discussion boards and news sites include a place to sell your domains. A few examples include:

- www.namepros.com
- www.domainstate.com
- www.dnforum.com

See the Appendix section for a full list of domaining forums.

Direct

Depending on your style you can cut out the middle man and sell directly to potential buyers via several different methods. You most likely have a good idea of the kind of people that would be interested in buying your domain name. Therefore, you can go to them directly to offer the sale of your domain. You can use tools such as Whois.com to find potential buyers.

You can also use DomainMart. You can perform searches that return businesses related to your domain name. All you really need to get hold of is an e-mail address so you can send a potential buyer a message.

Another readily available set of tools you can use to find potential buyers are search engines such as Google and Yahoo! Just type in the keywords associated with your domain name (for example, sports equipment) and then use the sponsored Adwords ads (usually on the right of the search results) to find the contact information for the companies you are targeting.

In addition you can go through the first and second page results and look at the URLs of the websites that come up. Many sites will not have great domain names or matching domain names optimized for the keywords, so they are good prospects to contact.

Once you have a potential buyer flagged you can put together your message. Be sure to include the following information:

- Benefits of buying your domain name
- The potential profits

- Sale price
- Your contact information

As well as contacting people for direct sales you may also get "walk-ins"; those that stumble across your domain name when searching or looking for sites similar to yours. No matter how a potential buyer finds you, always negotiate for the best price. Negotiation skill and acquisition urgency play an important role in selling domain names and, depending on your own level of experience, you may want to retain a broker to act on your behalf. You should also consider an impromptu auction, as you can expect at least one bidder. Weigh the benefits and limitations of each option before you decide on the best method for you.

Types Of Payments Accepted For Domain Sales

Selling your domain involves a successful payment followed by transferring the domain to the new owner. There are several payment types that you can accept, and knowing about them can make the difference between an easy transaction and a difficult (or an impossible) one.

The safest option is to use an Escrow service, as this ensures integrity and accuracy between buyer and seller. There is a small fee for using the Escrow service, which makes it mostly worthwhile when selling more expensive domains, as the high amount you will receive from your domain sale will easily offset the Escrow transaction fees.

It is well worth choosing this option when your domain sells for several hundred dollars or a 4 digit figure.

For smaller domain sales accepting Paypal is more than enough, however a note of caution with accepting echecks from Paypal: echecks take a few days to clear, which means that the whole transaction will be delayed. If domain flipping is a main source of income, echecks can really slow down and hinder the entire process for each domain you are selling.

Creating an Investment Strategy

The complex world of domain name investing can be intimidating for beginners. This chapter is intended to help you gain perspective.

If you are new to domaining, unfortunately you have arrived relatively late in the game. The initial wave of domain name investing, sometimes referred to as the Great Domain Gold Rush, was essentially over several years ago and the vast majority of the absolute best domains were scooped up by early investors. However, just because the rush is over doesn't mean the domaining industry is.

The successful domainers during the "rush" were people that had the presence of mind to take advantage of the early opportunities in the field of domain name investing. Their initiative and business acumen, or in some cases their pure good luck, paid off in spades. These people saw the opportunity that the vast majority of people failed to see and they were rewarded handsomely. Today, even though the rush is over, it is still the ability to see opportunities that others overlook that can turn you into a successful domainer.

Despite the boom days being over there is still good news for new domainers. Because of long keyphrase relevant domain names you have a second chance to get in on the domaining action. Thousands of good keyphrase names are available and in that sense the process of buying and selling domain names is better than it used to be.

Re-sale prices are now higher than during the "rush". Increased interest in the Internet has sent domain prices to an all-time high. Run-of-the-mill names commonly sell for $3,000 to $10,000 and better names sell for tens or hundreds of thousands of dollars.

Domains names are also now easier to sell. Many domain brokerage sites now exist to facilitate the sale of names. They attract buyers and provide appraisal and escrow services.

Your Domain Name Investment Strategy

Before you whip out your credit card and start buying domain names take the time to develop a personal investment strategy that outlines what your goals and intentions are. Smart people will want to do this with the help of one or more experienced AND successful domainers who might agree to serve as advisers. Choosing advisers and mentors is a very important step for new domain name investors. You will find that there are countless people on the various domaining related forums willing to offer free advice, but be vigilant not to take instruction from people who in fact may be entirely unqualified to offer it.

To establish your personal domain name investment strategy you must think carefully about your knowledge of your various target industries or niches, your financial resources, your tolerance for risk and your investment objectives. With those things in mind, you will be able to begin the process of selecting the right categories and types of domain names to invest in and the right mix of assets to meet your financial goals.

Establish Your Investment Objectives

What do you need from you investment portfolio, and when do you need it?

As mentioned towards the beginning of this book, you cannot work towards your goals until you know what they are. Your first step as a potential domain name investor should be to decide what you want to accomplish with your money, and when you want to accomplish it.

You may have many financial goals, e.g. to make a down payment on a house in two years, to help pay for your children's education in ten years, and to prepare for your retirement fifteen years after that. You might already be retired and simply want your money to earn a reasonable return and provide a reliable source of income for many years to come. Whatever your situation, take a few minutes to sit down and think about where you are now financially, where you want to be in the future and how investing in domain names is going to help you reach your goals.

Understand Your Tolerance for Risk

Your domain name investment strategy will also be affected by the way you are able to deal with risk, i.e. your risk tolerance.

In the investment world there is a direct relationship between expected returns and risk; the higher the expected payback from your investment, the higher the risk. Before you can decide on a personal investment strategy you must consider how much or how little risk you are prepared to take with your money. Your risk tolerance can be affected by the considerations below.

Time horizons

The amount of time you have to meet your financial goals and to make up for any losses you might experience. People with long time horizons may be more willing to endure periodic fluctuations in the value of their investments, or to adopt a "buy and hold" strategy.

Cash requirements

The extent to which you depend on your investments to meet day-to-day expenses. Investors who rely on their investments to meet daily living expenses will be much less able to tolerate any substantial losses.

Emotional factors

Your emotional response to risk and to changes in the value of your investments. Some people are quite comfortable with the ups and downs of the market, while others lose sleep when their investments fluctuate in value. Domaining is about establishing freedom in your life, not increasing your blood pressure, so consider the type of lifestyle you want to build.

There is no 'right' answer to the question, "How much risk should I take?" Risk tolerance is a personal issue. You should never feel obliged or pressured to take more investment risk than you are comfortable with. Remember though, that there is virtually no such thing as a high return risk free investment. As a general rule, you cannot expect to be rewarded with high returns on your investments if you are not able to accept the risks that go with them.

Diversity: Don't put all your eggs in one basket!

Every investment industry has its own inherent risks and domaining is not an exception. Investing in certain types of domain names can be highly speculative and extremely risky while other types can be of lesser risk with a more predictable outcome. Performance of different domains will be subject to varying levels of influence from current events, business and lifestyle trends, scientific and technical breakthroughs and a host of other factors.

For most domain name investors, what is important is the risk profile of their overall investment portfolio. By investing in a diverse portfolio of domain names you can reduce your overall risk. Diversification simply means not putting all your investment eggs in one basket. It is one of the key principles that every investor should understand clearly and implement consistently.

Choose the Right Asset Mix

When you begin to implement your personal investment strategy one of the first things you and your financial advisers must decide on is the asset mix you will put into your portfolio. There are three basic categories of investment products or assets: equity investments, debt investments, and cash or cash equivalents. The combination of these three types of products in a portfolio is called the asset mix.

The asset mix that you choose will be important in establishing the overall risk and the expected returns of your portfolio. Allocating your money among the three types of investments is another way to diversify your portfolio and ensure you are getting the best return for the level of risk you are taking.

While many investors focus on the performance of specific investments, it is generally agreed that the overall asset mix in a portfolio has the biggest impact on long-term results.

The right asset mix will depend on your investment objectives. Asset mix is an important part of your personal investment strategy and should be explored in great detail with your financial advisers.

Recognize the Limits of Your Investment Knowledge

Before investing your hard earned money in domain names you should assess your own knowledge of and experience in this field. Be honest with yourself. If you are reading this book you are most likely not an experienced domainer and therefore you must exercise caution when deciding on your approach to this business. Avoid domain name investment strategies you don't fully understand. If you have questions about a specific domain name investment or strategy, seek advice before you make your decision.

As mentioned previously, if you would like to improve your domain name investment knowledge, many domain related forums exist where one can learn and receive advice from other domainers. Of course you are ultimately responsible for the outcome of your domain name investments, so apply your own process of logic and reason when receiving advice on an internet forum from people whose expertise you cannot verify.

Do Your Homework

It's been said that some people do more research before buying a new television than they do before investing their life savings. Successful domain name investing requires extensive time and effort. That time and effort may be spent doing your own investment research. It should also be spent carefully selecting your financial advisers, consulting with them, and reviewing their recommendations.

Do's and Don'ts of Domain Name investing

- DO Establish clear and reasonable investment goals before you invest in domain names.

- DO Seek advice from various sources and ensure that they have the qualifications and experience required to offer sound advice.

- DO Remember that there is risk involved when investing in domain names. Don't take risks you can't afford or aren't comfortable with.

- DO Diversify your domain name investment portfolio to decrease your overall risk.

- DO Acknowledge the limits of your knowledge and conduct detailed study and analysis of the domain name industry. Avoid investing in areas you don't understand.

- DO Conduct precise "due diligence" prior to committing your hard earned money to an investment in domain names. Be sure you know what you are investing in and what impact it will have on the risk, potential returns and marketability of your domain name portfolio.

- DON'T Invest on the basis of hot tips and rumors, which historically have proven to be inaccurate or invalid.

- DON'T Blindly follow investment advice that you don't understand. This is especially true of the advice you may receive from the various domaining related internet forums. Recognize that there is a large variance in the level of experience and sophistication among the many posters on these forums and you should exercise caution when receiving guidance or advice from well-meaning people who may not have the actual experience they claim to have, etc.

• DON'T Be afraid to say NO to the suggestions of your advisors or mentors if you are not convinced the investments are right for you.

An essential adjunct to this investment guide is the article "A Long Hard Look at Domain Name Valuations," which paints a realistic picture of the changing playing field that domain name owners find themselves facing compared even to just a couple of years ago. If you haven't read the article yet, you can find it at igoldrush.com. This website contains a lot of great information that can increase your overall knowledge on domaining.

Whether you're considering purchasing new or existing domain names for investment, it's important to focus on how you're actually going to make money from your portfolio of domains. Without a clear up-front vision of the "path to liquidity" for your domain investments, it's better to stay out of the investment side of the business entirely.

Remember, a domain name that is gathering virtual dust, i.e. that's not generating revenue or at least traffic, is worth nothing at all. In fact, it has a negative worth as you'll be required to pay a renewal fee every year to maintain the registration. On the other hand, it only takes a small amount of revenue to make your domains profitable. As long as a domain name pays for its own upkeep over the course of a year, there's nothing to stop you holding on to it until you feel the best time to sell arrives.

Common Mistakes to Avoid

"Those who do not learn from history are doomed to repeat it."

- George Santayana

People who are new to any business or industry are often prone to repeating the mistakes made by those who have preceded them. In most instances these mistakes, some of which may literally be very costly, can be avoided by taking the time to research and self-educate.

Registering Low Quality Domain Names

Most experienced domainers agree that the most common mistake made by newbies is registering of low quality domain names. Most domainers, myself included, look back at some of their early registrations and admit that they could not have been more wrong in their estimation of the quality of some of these domain names. You do not have to repeat our mistakes.

However, you do have to accept the fact that you'll find practically all of the attractive .com domain names you can think of have already been registered by someone else. Accepting this fact is critical to your success as a domainer because until you do so you will be tempted to register numerous variations of good domain names that are already registered by adding a word or two, or a hyphen to the .com version. You might also register the .info or .biz version of the domain without stopping to ponder why the 'dumb' owner of the .com version failed to register this 'gold mine'!

The main point to remember is that if what seems like a prominent .com domain name is available there is a significant chance is has already been considered and rejected by a large number of experienced domainers. You would be wise to slow down and reflect on why the name is still available. With experience, you will be able to spot some of the reasons why seasoned domainers have not registered the name and you will avoid wasting money and learning the hard way.

Before you register any domain name you must ask yourself if anyone would ever buy it from you, or if anyone would ever realistically type the name into their Web browser or a search engine. These questions, if answered honestly, will go a long way in ensuring that you do not make impulsive decisions when buying domain names. Recognizing good domain names takes experience that can only be obtained by educating yourself via various sources such this book, news stories and articles, information found on domaining related web forums and through the advice and guidance of experienced domainers who frequent these forums.

Don't fall into the common trap of registering domain names before you know what you are doing. Registrations are not expensive but rookies tend to make mistakes in volume and often register dozens of worthless domain names before they learn they have made some classic mistakes and wasted hundreds of dollars in the process. Before you invest your money take the time to do your homework.

Failing to Master the Tools Used by Professional Domainers

If you were entering a highly skilled profession, such as carpentry for example, you would probably observe experienced proponents so you could become aware of their techniques and best practices. You would surely ask for their opinions on the various tools required to be an effective carpenter and for recommendations of the best dealers from which to purchase these tools. Sounds like common sense, right? Unfortunately amongst brand new domain name investors common sense is not always common.

For various reasons domaining attracts people who, through a lack of knowledge of the topic, embark on a course of undisciplined and illogical registration of domain names that are essentially worthless. This is entirely avoidable through using some of the same tools professional domainers employ. Do yourself a huge favor and take advantage of the many domaining related forums that exist and ask the experienced "carpenters" about the tools of this business. You'll be amazed at the amount of knowledge and advice they will freely offer you.

Sadly, many neophyte domainers remain ignorant of these tools and waste a great amount of time and money. Self-inflicted ignorance of the tools used by professional domainers ensures that many newbies will flail about the domain name industry as ineffectively as a boxer trying to fight his opponent while blindfolded; expending much energy but accomplishing very little, if anything at all. The very fact that you purchased this book indicates that you are aware you need to self-educate and the chances of you becoming one of the blindfolded domainers swinging wildly at one worthless domain name after another will be greatly reduced if you follow the advice contained on these pages.

Proper use of the most effective tools will enable you to maximize your chances of success and minimize costly mistakes. Of course, the best tools are domaining related knowledge and experience, both of which beginners obviously lack. If you are just starting or you are someone who has not fared well so far, you have to immerse yourself in the study of this business in order to succeed. Knowledge and mastery of the tools is a great place to begin your education.

Becoming a Victim of a Thief or Scam Artist

The domain name industry is, unfortunately, fertile ground for thieves and con artists. Most victims are beginners and the crooks prey almost exclusively on them. One of the most common scams is the "domain name appraisal" con, where you are contacted by a seemingly interested buyer who insists on an appraisal performed by an appraiser of his choice. Eager to make the sale, you agree to the appraisal, pay for it via your credit card and await the results. After waiting for days, you realize that the buyer and appraiser were in cahoots with each other and your money is gone.

The domain name business is largely conducted via the Internet and e-mail. It is quite common for domainers to buy and sell domain names to and from people they do not know, so it is important to conduct transactions securely. One way to ensure that a transaction is safely conducted is to use an escrow service. This tactic will scare most scammers away and you should plan to use it most if not all of the time.

New scams are continuously surfacing and you should review related discussions on domaining related web forums. You can stay aware of the many scams and tactics used by the unsavory parasites on our business by frequenting domaining related forums and reading the stories of those who let their guard down and became victims. The main point to remember is that when dealing with any transaction to make sure you cover yourself for any possible risks and do your due diligence on any buyer. A buyer or seller may try to convince you they are "trustworthy". Ignore these tactics. Whether they are trustworthy or not is irrelevant. Business is business and every transaction should be made securely and "by the book" regardless of who is involved and how "trustworthy" they tell you they are.

Failing to Understand That You Can Lose Money in Domaining

Chances are that many people who read this book have become aware of the domain name industry by reading an article in a newspaper or magazine that told of the vast wealth attained by several of the more successful professional domainers. Invariably, these accounts either state or imply that domaining is a business in which money literally streams into your bank account while you play golf all day or sit beside the pool behind your mansion in Miami Beach! I have good news and bad news.

First, the good news. If you study the domain name business and educate yourself in its nuances, as professionals have studied their specific business, you can indeed attain significant financial success. This is not an easy business to master and it will be a good while before you will be able to honestly say that you are an experienced domainer, much less a professional. However, if you stay with it and do sufficient research your chances of making a profit in this business are good.

Now for the not so good news. A lot of people lose money in this business. For every successful domainer who is the subject of the stories cited above there are hundreds of people who are sitting on dozens or even hundreds of domain names that are as useless as ice cubes in the Arctic Circle! Of course, this is something that is rarely, if ever, mentioned in the articles. Nobody likes to think of failure and we rarely consider that we may fail at something, but the fact is that you can lose money in this business. If you insist on going off half-cocked and registering domain names before you know what you are doing, YOU WILL LOSE MONEY IN THIS BUSINESS! Additionally, if you see domaining as a business in which the profits come easy and the associated work load is minimal, you are in for a very unpleasant experience.

Some Rules for Newbies

Rule # 1: You don't know what you don't know. First, find out what you need to learn, then set about learning it.

Rule # 2: In the domain name business, experience is the best teacher but it is also the most expensive way of learning! Build your experience but do so with effective risk management.

Rule # 3: Don't just be in the business, BE OF THE BUSINESS! Immerse yourself in learning everything you can so you can make increasingly better decisions.

Rule # 4: Even if you do not intend to become a professional domainer, you must still do the same things as the professionals or you will lose money in this business!

Rule # 5: Don't confuse enthusiasm with capability, either in yourself or those advising you. Be realistic about your own experience and that of the people you listen to.

Developments in the Domaining World

As you start moving into building your experience with domain name investments, remember not to rest on your laurels even when you start to enjoy success. With the business of domaining one thing is certain; the opportunities for profit will continue to change and evolve constantly as each day goes by. Remember that during the "rush" in the early days of the internet there was no common concept of "domaining". The people that were highly successful at that time saw a new opportunity emerging. While others were battling to connect their dial up modems for the first time, these pioneer domainers were already seeing ten years into the future. They watched patterns, monitored developments and hence were effectively able to predict the future. Today, it is that same ability to keep your finger on the pulse of changes in the domaining world that will lead to your success.

As mentioned many times throughout this book, make it your business to pay attention to the various domaining web forums. Join, ask questions, and above all read, read, read. Remember that the world of domaining is not in a bubble, it is directly tied to what is going on around us. Watch for emerging trends in industry and society look for ways to capitalize on them. Our earlier example of the site netbooks.com shows how watching for new products that are set to become popular can be very lucrative.

Spend some time searching the internet for blogs and news sites relevant to domaining. You'll find that many prominent and successful domainers are very open with sharing what is going on in with their investments and you may find information they post that literally translates to pure gold. Find sites that sit well with your own style of communication and learning, bookmark them, and visit them often. There are also a number of sites you can monitor to help you keep up to date with major changes in the domaining world:

- www.dailychanges.com
- www.zooknic.com
- www.domaintools.com
- www.domebase.com
- www.webhosting.info

- www.domainpond.com
- www.registrarstats.com
- www.cookreport.com
- www.dnjournal.com

Stay vigilant of what is going on in the world around you, diversify your portfolio and manage your risk, apply yourself to absorbing every piece of information you can and your success in the world of domaining is well on its way.

Appendix : Domaining Resources

You can refer to this section for a wealth of domain resources that will help manage your new business. I highly suggest that you take advantage of this list, which includes some of the following types of information:

- Domain discussion boards
- Website ranking and traffic
- Link popularity sites
- Domain trends
- Word list, keyword tools and search engine tools
- Expiring domain sites and drop catching services
- Domain Registrars
- Domain Marketplaces
- Legal Research and general domaining news
- Domain Parking Services and advertising revenue services
- Site development and webmaster tools
- Payment/ Escrow Services
- Programming And Freelancing Services

Domaining Discussion Forums

- www.namepros.com
- www.dnforum.com
- www.domainstate.com
- www.acorndomains.co.uk for the UK market
- www.dnc.ca for the Canadian market
- www.dntrade.com.au for the Australian market

WHOIS Lookups

- www.internic.net
- www.uwhois.com
- www.freewho.com
- www.whois-search.com
- www.iwhois.com
- www.whoissoft.com
- www.domainsearch.com
- www.domainwhitepages.com

Link Popularity

- www.alexa.com
- www.ranking.com
- www.startname.com
- www.linkpopularity.com

- www.pagerank.net/link-popularity-checker

Domain Appraisals

- www.valuate.com
- www.estibot.com
- domainindex.com
- www.domainappraisal.org
- www.networksolutions.com
- www.instica.com

Word Lists/ Domain Searching Tools

- www.acronymfinder.com
- www.wordlist.sourceforge.net
- www.wordspy.com
- www.net-comber.com
- www.namedroppers.com
- www.nametumbler.com
- www.nameboy.com
- www.merriam-webster.com
- www.zfbot.com
- www.lazymate.com
- www.namestall.com

Expiring Domain Lists

- www.pool.com
- www.expireddomains.net
- www.snapcheck.com
- www.deleteddomains.com
- www.domainpond.com
- www.justdropped.com
- www.whois-search.com
- www.exody.com
- www.domainsbot.com
- www.dnslocator.com
- www.pddw.com
- www.genericdomainfinder.com
- www.freshavails.com

Drop Catching Services

- www.pool.com
- www.namejet.com
- www.dropping.com
- www.snapnames.com
- www.enom.com
- www.dropcatcher.co.uk
- www.godaddy.com
- www.domainmonster.com

- www.devaid.com
- www.dropping.ca
- www.domainrecover.net

Keyword/Search Engine Tools

- https://adwords.google.com/ko/KeywordPlanner/Home
- http://google.com/insights/search
- http://www.google.com/trends/
- http://www.google.com/intl/en/zeitgeist/
- freekeywords.wordtracker.com
- www.keywordeye.com
- www.keywordspy.com
- www.Semrush.com

Wait List Service (WLS)

- www.icann.org
- www.enom.com

Registries (NICs)

- www.verisigninc.com
- www.afilias.info
- www.denic.de

- www.cira.ca
- www.iana.org
- www.marcaria.com
- www.domain.re

Domain Registrars

- www.godaddy.com
- www.enom.com
- www.dotregistrar.com
- www.dotster.com
- www.mydomain.com
- www.fabulous.com
- www.namecheap.com
- www.1and1.com
- www.dynadot.com
- www.fxdomains.com
- www.targetdomain.com
- www.dona.com

Domain Marketplaces

- www.afternic.com
- www.aftermarket.com
- www.pool.com

- www.sedo.com
- www.flippa.com
- www.dnforum.com
- www.domainstate.com
- www.namepros.com
- www.cax.com
- www.premierportfolio.com

Larger Domain Marketeers

- www.buydomains.com
- www.dotcomagency.com
- www.classicnames.com
- www.eyename.com

Advertising/Revenue

- www.ppcincome.com
- www.adwords.google.com
- www.google.com/adsense
- www.kanoodle.com
- www.clickbank.com
- www.cj.com
- www.payperclicksearchengines.com
- www.shareasale.com

Parking Services

- www.ppcincome.com
- www.aftermarket.com
- www.sedo.com
- www.Godaddy.com/parking/domain-name-parking.aspx
- www.parklogic.com
- www.parkingcrew.com
- www.domainsponsor.com
- www.domainparking.com
- www.trafficz.com
- www.namedrive.com

DNS (routing) Services

- www.zoneedit.com
- www.dyndns.com
- www.easydns.com

Legal Research

- www.uspto.gov
- www.strategis.ic.gc.ca
- www.chillingeffects.org
- www.domains.org
- www.arbiter.wipo.int

- www.domainfight.net
- www.dnforum.com
- www.moniker.com
- www.dnjournal.com

Domain Trends/News/Education

- www.dailychanges.com
- www.zooknic.com
- www.domebase.com
- www.webhosting.info
- www.domainpond.com
- www.domainersmagazine.com
- www.registrarstats.com
- www.cookreport.com
- www.verisigninc.com
- www.dnjournal.com
- www.domaining.com
- www.domainnames3d.com
- www.emergingdomains.com
- www.destinysweb.com
- www.hallofshame.com
- www.domainsherpa.com
- www.descriptivedomainnames.com
- www.namescon.com

- targetedtraffic.com

Web site Rankings/Traffic

- www.domaintools.com
- www.alexa.com
- www.compete.com

Site Development

- www.minisites.com
- www.steadyniche.com

Payment/Escrow Services

- www.paypal.com
- www.2checkout.com
- www.escrow.com
- www.ecop.com

Tools for Domainers/Webmasters

- www.webmaster-toolkit.com
- www.cleverforward.com
- www.bravenet.com

- www.templatemonster.com
- www.animationfactory.com
- www.google.com/webmasters/tools
- www.smartling.com
- www.dudamobile.com

Scripts for Domains

- www.dropscripts.com
- www.desktopapi.com
- www.checkurl.info
- www.domainsaide.com
- dnresult.com

Programming and Freelancing Services

- www.freelancer.com
- www.guru.com
- www.elance.com
- www.odesk.com

Printed in Great Britain
by Amazon